NO BANANA SPLITS

BUILDING LIFELONG DISCIPLES
IN A SHORT TERM WORLD

Bob Perkins

BRIGHTON PUBLISHING LLC
435 N. HARRIS DRIVE
MESA, AZ 85203

NO BANANA SPLITS

BUILDING LIFELONG DISCIPLES
IN A SHORT TERM WORLD

BOB PERKINS

BRIGHTON PUBLISHING LLC
435 N. HARRIS DRIVE
MESA, AZ 85203
WWW.BRIGHTONPUBLISHING.COM

ISBN13: 978-1-62183-342-0
ISBN 10: 1-62183-342-9

PRINTED IN THE UNITED STATES OF AMERICA

First Edition

COVER DESIGN: TOM RODRIGUEZ

Acknowledgements

As with my previous book, Building A Vision For Your Life, a great number of people have contributed to the thoughts in this book. It would be impossible to mention all of the kids, leaders, staff, and committee people who have been essential in making this book a reality, but I would like to highlight a few.

First, none of this would have been possible without the greatest woman in the world by my side. My wife Debbie has been a true partner in every sense of the word. She is better with kids than anyone I've ever known, is an inspiration to leaders, a model for staff and a true friend to our "adult" community. She is a fantastic mother to our boys and has been adventurous enough to go on this journey with me. She read, edited and contributed to this book in countless ways and her impact is on every page. I cannot imagine doing this ride with anyone else and I am thankful beyond measure to the Lord for His gift of her in my life. I love you hun!

TO MY MENTORS:

Jerry Johnson—who was my Young Life leader, my first boss, told me to "marry her!" and understood the "block and tackling" of Young Life better than anyone. He patiently shared his wisdom with me. Thank you!

Newt Hetrick—who was the Area Director in Baltimore when I was a volunteer leader. He gave me the opportunity to lead my first club and I learned how to be an Area Director from him. Thank you.

Hal Merwald—who performed our marriage ceremony, cared for us when we were damaged goods, gave me the opportunity to run the race in Canada and helped me navigate a different culture. Thank you!

Dr. Paul Kooistra—who was President of Covenant Theological Seminary while I was a student there and was willing to meet with me monthly, patiently helping me process the theological deep end of the pool. He is an inspiration to me. Thank You!

To my sister Debbie. My first "girl leader" who was there when it all started and who passed at far too young (fifty-two). I have thought of her every time I work on this book and miss her every day.

To the men who gathered for my sixtieth birthday. You know who you are. This book is for you, because it has always been about you. Thank you for letting me love you.

Bryan and Taylor: Thanks for letting daddy go to the high school. I am eternally grateful for you and proud of you every day.

Don McGuire and the team at Brighton—thanks for putting up with the endless edits and "conversations" over the cover. Thanks for taking this book to the next level.

Jesus—He loves me, this I know, because the Bible tells me so. I am weak, but He is strong. Thank you!

ᐃPreface to the 2016 Editionᐃ

I never imagined that No Banana Splits would have the impact it has had or would still be used as a resource twenty years after it was first written. I continue to be amazed that I still get phone calls and e-mails from all over the country from people ordering copies of this book. I am grateful to each and every one of you, and I appreciate your affirmation more than you know.

Since its first format—twelve pages handed in as an assignment—I have gone back several times and rewritten parts, most notably when I was in Ontario and the book was being used by the Canadian staff as a training tool. I have often thought of going back and updating the book, sending it to my publisher, and getting it legitimately published but have put that off to focus on other projects—most notably my book, Building A Vision for Your Life.

A couple of months ago, I was sitting with a staff person and we were talking about "beginning with the end in mind," the phrase made famous by Stephen Covey in his book, The Seven Habits of Highly Effective People. I realized as we talked that this is the key concept of No Banana Splits.

The entire premise of No Banana Splits is based on the concept of beginning with the "end in mind." I grew up in a wonderful Christian family, attended a great church and became a Christian in seventh grade at church camp. I was totally involved in church and Young Life—never missing Club meetings, Campaigners, weekend camps, a week at Frontier Ranch, youth group, and church on Sunday—throughout my high school years. If ever there was a kid who was going to walk with Christ the rest of his life, it should have been me.

But by the time I graduated from college, I was barely hanging on to my faith,[i] and most of the Christian friends I had known through Young Life had walked away from the faith altogether. As I put my life back together and eventually became a volunteer leader, I wanted a different "end in mind." The kids that would come though my Young Life Club had to be better equipped to go on in the faith than I was. The "end in mind" had to be that a kid would walk in the faith for his/her entire life; and as leaders, we had a responsibility to do everything we could to facilitate that end.

I had been a Christian "taker," and for all my taking, all the Bible studies, camp trips, and fellowship, I was barely a follower of Christ in my life. There had to be a better way—a better experience for Christian kids (or adults for that matter) to have that would equip them to walk with Christ their entire lives.

The "end in mind" became that kids would walk with Christ their entire lives, would go on to be Christian husbands and wives, Christian fathers and mothers, Christian business people, pastors and missionaries. When I looked back on my ministry, I would see men and women who were walking with Christ years and years after they had come through my Club.

What I didn't know was how radical this idea would be. I didn't know that it would fly in the face of much of the thinking of those in the ministry with me. A senior staff person for whom I have the highest respect once told me, "We minister to a passing parade." He meant what I have come to realize is the common thinking:

The end in mind is that a kid stands up at the "say-so"[ii] and that's it. That's the end. Once a kid makes a profession of faith, we are done and we move on to the next kid.

A senior staff person once asked me about my strategy, and I told him that I liked to work with kids when they were freshmen in high school, because then we had three more years to disciple them before they went off to college. The senior staff person disagreed with me (pretty vehemently) and said that "No, our strategy had to be to take seniors to camp because it was their last chance to hear the Gospel." Even disregarding the horrendous theological problem that presents and the arrogance of thinking that the only opportunity a kid has to hear the Gospel is at our camp, this position inherently suggests that the correct strategy is for a kid to meet Christ after his or her senior year, weeks later he or she goes off to college, and then we wash our hands of that relationship and that is somehow a good thing.

The root problem is a two-tiered theological one. On one tier of the problem is that we have no responsibility for disciple making, and the second tier of the problem is that the act of standing up at a "say-so" or praying a prayer is the guarantee of salvation. It is worth noting that the Bible never speaks of converts, only of disciples, and that the Bible never gives us a formulaic prayer for salvation—but more on that later in the book.

There is something else, another mystery. In the twenty years that I served in the ministry, in the four different areas (Baltimore, Maryland, Bethlehem, Pennsylvania, St. Louis, Missouri, and Ontario, Canada) and in a mix of different cultures (Northeast, Midwest, and Canadian) the principles, strategy, and methodology encompassed in this book worked. We had bigger Clubs, took more kids to camp, and had better "end in mind" (kids continuing to walk with Christ, not only through their college years but also into adulthood) than most everyone else in comparable places. We had the biggest Club in Baltimore, the biggest Club in the Northeast, the biggest Club in the Midwest, and the biggest Club in Canada. Yet instead of widespread acceptance of these principles, the idea was only embraced by a few.

It reminds me of when an interviewer asked the president of Southwest Airlines why the other legacy airlines hadn't followed Southwest. She shook her head and said she didn't know but thought they thought it was beneath them. My guess is that it's something like that—but I don't really know. I don't know why anyone would devote their lives to seeing kids stand up at a say-so when they could instead give their lives to seeing kids walk with Christ their entire lives. It remains a mystery to me.

No Banana Splits is written to help you have a ministry that begins with the idea that a sovereign God has called you to be His leader in the lives of kids, that they will know and walk with Christ their entire lives and at the ultimate end of the day both you and they will hear the words, "Well done good and faithful servant."

Introduction

In the fall of 1971, the girl next door invited me to Young Life. As a sophomore in high school, I was thrilled at the thought of going anywhere with a junior female! I remember that night as if it happened yesterday. Sitting on the floor of a crowded living room, I experienced my first Young Life Club. It was wonderful—the singing, the skit, the talk, the people—everything about it was fantastic. Over the next three years, I went to Club and Campaigners every week, attended all the weekend camps, and spent a week at Frontier Ranch in Colorado.

After graduating from college, I knew I wanted to get involved with Young Life as a leader. As I began to reflect on my own Young Life experiences, my time in college struggling with the faith, and the Biblical principles regarding discipleship, I was convinced of the Biblical mandate to "make disciples" rather than simply converts and I wanted to do so in the context of Young Life.

During my first volunteer leadership experience with a Club in Baltimore, Maryland, I began experimenting with a different approach from the one I had experienced in high school. While the Club retained the same elements I had loved about that first Young Life Club I attended, my work with Campaigners was different. In my first staff assignment in Bethlehem, Pennsylvania, I built upon what I had learned in Baltimore and continued to expand the role and importance of Campaigners in my ministry. In St. Louis, Missouri, I had the opportunity to apply those same principles on a larger scale. God continued to affirm a commitment to the Campaigner-centered ministry you will read about in these pages and blessed us with eight great years in St. Louis. In 1996, I moved to Canada, and I took on the role of Ontario director for Young Life Canada. Again we saw this model continue to bear fruit, not only in Ontario but also in numerous places across Canada.

This book represents the thoughts and processes of many people and reflects their valuable input over more than twenty years of using the Campaigner-centered model. By reading it, I hope you will catch a sense of our commitment to Christ, our desire to be obedient to Him in all we do and see Him proclaimed to the world, and our continuing love for high school kids.

The purpose of this book is to outline a perspective on ministry. Before beginning the outline, however, an awareness of two important points is critical in understanding the rest of this book. First, ministry flows out of what God is doing in us. Ministry should be an outpouring of what Christ is doing in us, and who He is making us to be each day. We cannot be different people in our ministerial roles than we are in our daily walks with Christ. Everything else we do becomes an empty program if it does not stem from a living, growing, personal relationship with Christ.

Second, we cannot be about building our kingdom. Francis Schaeffer said, "Most men want to build their own kingdom. Some men want to build God's kingdom for him. Only a few men want God to build His kingdom through them."

May we be the people God uses to build His Kingdom.

The Approach

In developing a basis for ministry, the following approach will be used. First, we will start with laying the Biblical, theological foundation necessary for building a solid ministry. Second, from that Biblical/theological base, we will develop a philosophical foundation from which we will operate. Third, after establishing our Biblical/theological and philosophical perspectives, we will look at the functions—that which our ministry is supposed to accomplish in its broadest aspects. Finally, we will consider several forms, which flow from the function of our ministry.

If we were to compare this approach to a building, the Biblical/theological foundation would be the rock bed on which we would anchor our building, the philosophical basis would be the foundation of the building, the function would be the structural supports for the building, and the form would be the outward appearance of the building itself. The casual observer would see only the outward appearance, but the other parts of the structure are what hold the entire edifice together. And so it is with our ministry. The casual observer may only see Clubs, camps, Campaigners, etc., but there must be an underlining infrastructure that holds all of this together.

GRAPHICALLY STATED:

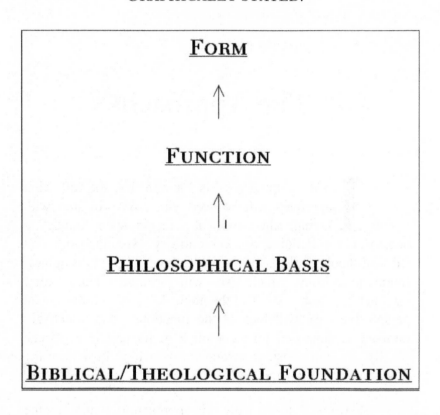

Chapter One

BIBLICAL/THEOLOGICAL FOUNDATION

I n this chapter, I will focus on our understanding of and the necessity for a solid Biblical foundation for our lives and ministry. We live in a world that is Biblical illiterate and even most Christians do not have a basic understanding of solid Biblical theology. It is my view that all ministry, should flow from proper Biblical conviction, understanding, and application. We obey God's will in ministry only when we view the Scripture as our "God-breathed" source of guidance and direction. It is through His Word that God has chosen to communicate His truths to us. To reject His Word is to reject His truth and rejection of God's Word leads to confusion, defeat, and even disobedience.

In the first half of this century, a common paradigm for Christian organizations was the military. For example, Young Life has "Campaigners" (Bible studies) after the concept of a military campaign. Campus Crusade for Christ is referenced to

1

a military crusade, and the Navigators is a reference to a ship's navigator.

It is trendy today to think and look to the business community as models for the latest in management techniques. We attempt to follow large corporations with their management consultants and expertise and apply those principles to our Christian organizations. It is not that these philosophies are necessarily wrong; in fact, there is much we can learn from them. The problem is, however, that secular wisdom, no matter how attractive or brilliant it may seem, cannot replace God's wisdom. A pastor friend of mine once said to me, "The problem with the elders in this church is that they think we should run the church the same way they run their businesses. The truth is they should run their businesses and the church based on the principles of Christ." As Christians, we are set apart to do God's work in God's way; and the only way we can know God's way is to know His Word.

Paul tells us in 1 Corinthians 1:25, "For the foolishness of God is wiser than men, and the weakness of God is stronger than men." We are called to follow the wisdom of God, which is wiser than anything man has ever dreamed of. That wisdom of God is revealed in the Bible.

In Matthew 7:24–27, Jesus tells us that the man who builds his house on His words is like the one who builds a house on rock. It will not be moved. To build a philosophy of ministry without Biblical foundation is to build our house upon the sand. It assumes human wisdom equips us better than God's Word for carrying out His will.

His truth will not be moved no matter where He places us in ministry. Whether we're in a more liberal or even post-

Christian culture or a conservative "Bible Belt" area of the world, God's Word is authoritative for all time and for all people.

As we consider a Biblical basis for our ministry, there are three specific areas we should consider. They are 1) the Biblical mandate for ministry, 2) the theological framework for evangelism, and 3) a brief theology of prayer.

THE BIBLICAL MANDATE
EVANGELISM IS OUR CALLING

As we look at the Scripture, we see there is a mandate for evangelism, which is present even in the Old Testament. We know God's purpose in selecting a people (or more accurately, in creating a people for Himself) is so that the world might see Him and His power displayed through His people.

You will remember that Paul tells us in Romans 9 that God raised up Pharaoh and hardened his heart for the purpose of God showing His power through him (that is Pharaoh). This was done so that not only the Egyptians and Jews of that time would see the power of God but also so that all the nations of the world would see God's power for ages to come. God's purpose was that all the people of the world would recognize him as the supreme creator and sustainer of all existence.

Additionally, we are told that Israel was given a mandate to tell the other nations about God. We see in their law the specific regulations for circumcising the non-Jew when he came into the fellowship of the Jews. This regulation was given because it was expected by God that His people would be a witness to the surrounding nations and those nations would be converted and join the fellowship. It was not

3

only the accidental assimilation of the non-Jew but also the anticipated and expected goal of God for His people to be involved in evangelism.

When we examine the New Testament, we see that Jesus commands us to make disciples of all the nations. His desire is not that we keep the Good News to ourselves but rather that we tell the world. This point is brought home dramatically when we see at the day of Pentecost the disciples miraculously speaking in the native languages of the many foreigners present. God's Spirit descended on the disciples and enabled them to speak the native tongue of the hearers, because it is the desire of God that the nations should hear the Gospel in their own "language."

A case could also be made that the divine purpose of the dispersion of the Jews to the surrounding areas outside of Jerusalem and even outside of the national boundaries of Israel was to prepare a foundation for the spread of the Gospel beyond the gates of the holy city.

There is no sense in the Bible that the purpose of God was for the Gospel to remain with those who already possess it.

In too many places in our North American version of Christianity, we have adopted a "walled city" approach to our faith. We have tried to insulate ourselves against the negative influences of the pagan culture around us. We have our own magazines, television and radio stations, our own vacation places where we can be with only other Christians, and we work hard at separating ourselves from the nonbelieving world around us. When I moved to Canada, I discovered that one of the big events for our church's youth group was "Christian night" at the roller rink. I asked some kids what made it Christian night and they told me that it was the night they played only Christian music and only other Christians came. I wondered then and now what has happened to us that we can't even roller skate with non-Christians. While the Gospel calls us to build bridges to the culture in order to share the truth with them, we are busy building walls to keep us separate from the culture.

God's desire for his people is that we are salt and light in the world, and it is incumbent upon us to build those bridges so that truth can be proclaimed to others as it has been to us.

DISCIPLES NOT CONVERTS

We should note here that the Biblical mandate is for disciples and not only converts. In the New Testament, there is never a mandate for conversions only, but rather the charge is always for disciples. The idea of a convert who was not a disciple was inconceivable to the New Testament Christian. Discipleship meant the following of the teaching of Jesus, and the devotion of one's life to Christ. It was not possible for a person to become a convert to Christianity without deciding at the same time to follow the teaching of Jesus and dedicate his or her life to following the Messiah. Today we have separated these two ideas and have people who claim to have had a conversion experience with Jesus but have not made the decision to follow Him or commit their lives to Him. This idea is not only outside the New Testament but also outside the early church.

As the early church grew beyond the sphere of Judaism, there was concern that the new believers did not have the same background of knowledge the initial members had regarding an understanding of the Scripture. In the early church, therefore, those who were interested in Christianity would be part of the fellowship of believers for up to three years before they were extended the privilege of baptism and the Lord's Supper.[iii] Because church membership brought with it the sting of persecution and possible death, it was a far more serious thing to be identified with the church. People considered this serious decision and its potential consequences knowing they were making a decision that would have dramatic consequences on their lives and the lives of their families. This was not merely making a verbal statement of "conversion" that could be forgotten at a later time. They were becoming disciples of Jesus with their lives not only their mouths. A simple prayer at the end of a tract would not be sufficient.

Have you ever wondered why "the sinner's prayer" is not in the Bible? If a simple formula prayer could have been recited that would have granted eternal life and been the demarcation point of conversion, then why isn't that prayer stated somewhere in the Bible? Why is it, that of all the people who were converted by the Apostle Paul in the book of Acts, not one of them was given "the sinner's prayer?" Or perhaps this is a better question: If there is no "sinner's prayer" in the Bible, then where did all those prayers at the end of evangelistic brochures come from? In every evangelical tract or book, there is a prayer somewhere near the end that guarantees the reader salvation if they will simply pray that prayer. So where did those prayers come from if not from the Bible? And what do they tell us about our theology of evangelism?

We need to look at the proper theological context for evangelism. Theology has not always enjoyed an honored place in our evangelical circles. We have wanted to "get on with the work of winning souls" and have looked suspiciously on theology as being, at best, too academic and irrelevant and, at worst, divisive. Regrettably, in our rush to expediency, we may have lost the basic principles of theological thought, which are needed in order to form a solid basis for our work. Theology—the study of God—is a good and necessary thing for those of us who are called to evangelism. We study the Word of God in order to understand what God is doing in the work of salvation and what responsibilities we have as His agents in that work.

DIVINE SOVEREIGNTY AND HUMAN RESPONSIBILITY

Therefore, before we go any further, we need to discern the Biblical perspective on divine sovereignty and human responsibility with regard to evangelism. In other words, we need to ask the questions, "What is God's job, what is my job as an evangelist, and what is the job of the person we are witnessing to?" when it comes to evangelism. It might be helpful to look at this in chart form.

If I were to take a sheet of paper and divide it into three columns with one column being titled "God's Job," another column titled "My Job," and a third column titled "Hearers Job," this is what it would look like.

God's Job—The Evangelist's Job—Man's Job

Let's begin by looking at God's side of the ledger.

I. GOD'S JOB

From the Scripture, what would we want to put on God's side of this ledger? We would want to begin with the idea that God is the one who calls people to Himself.

7

In John 6:44, Jesus tells us "no one can come to me unless the Father draws him." So we know that the action of being drawn to God comes from God and not from man. John also tells us that it is not that we have first loved Christ but that He first loved us. God is the initiator of our salvation. Our salvation begins with action on the part of God. On God's side of the ledger, we must begin with the idea that God draws or calls people to Himself.

In addition, we know that it is the job of the Holy Spirit to convict people of their sin (John 16:9). It is not the job of man to be convicted of his sin by his own good morals, because there is not enough goodness in man to accomplish such a feat. Because man has been born into sin, and is by nature a sinful creature, he is incapable of being convicted of his sin as a result of his own inner abilities. Therefore, we must conclude that it is God's job—not the job of any individual man—to convict men of sin. So we must add "God Convicts People of their Sin" to God's side of the ledger.

Walter Chantry, in his book titled Today's Gospel, Authentic or Synthetic, says that without the conviction of sin there is no repentance and without repentance there is no salvation. Salvation, therefore, is necessarily dependent upon God convicting us of our sin.

Therefore, since God is the one who convicts men of their sin and without the conviction of sin there is no repentance and thus no salvation, we must conclude that salvation is the supreme act of God who convicts people of their sin and draws them to Himself.

When discussing the inability of man to become convicted of his own sin and realizing that man is in a desperate state of utter inability to do anything other than sin, it is possible that some might interpret this as mankind having no value to God. In other words, some may say that if man is sinful, he cannot have value to God. Let's pause here to briefly discuss the value of sinful men in relation to their holy God.

THE VALUE OF SINFUL PEOPLE IN GOD'S ECONOMY

At this point you might be uncomfortable with the idea that we're not good people because you know that we are created in the image of God and that God loves us. Let me give an illustration of the difference between value and goodness, which might help clarify this distinction.

The National Museum in Florence, Italy, holds one of the most famous works of art in the entire world: Michelangelo's statue of David. It is an incredible work of sculpture that is both breathtaking and inspiring to all who view it. Every day crowds stand around the statue and stare in amazement at the incredible piece of marble that looks as if it will come to life at any second. To say that there is great attention to detail in the statue would be a gross understatement. The statue is both artistically stunning as well as anatomically perfect. The muscles are distinct, the blood vessels defined, and even the toenails appear real. It is arguably the most magnificent piece of art in the world!

[iv]When you go to see the David statute, you enter through a hallway that has on either side of it six or eight large blocks of marble that Michelangelo began to sculpt and quit. There are large pieces of marble with a head begun or an arm started or the beginning of a bust. Michelangelo began these works and stopped for some reason. They are not good works of art, but they are priceless because they are Michelangelo's. Their value comes from the one who made them not from

9

being good works of art. They are not good, but they are valuable; in fact they are priceless.

We are valuable because of the one who made us— God—not because we're good. We're not good but we are valuable. This is a key foundation principle. Our value is not based on what we do— we do bad things—but on the one who made us...God. Once we understand this, we can be free to admit that we're not good people, and we are free to throw ourselves on the mercy of God for forgiveness of our sin.

THE RELIGION OF HUMANISM

We live in a world that is confused. On one hand, we are told that we are all good people and capable of anything if we turn our will to whatever is our goal. You could be the next American Idol! The reality of course is that most of us cannot be the next American Idol, because most of us can't sing!

On the other hand, we value success like no other culture before us. We idolize the media-driven celebrities who live a life far distant from anything we can imagine, and we are bombarded daily with the idea that we are all equal, all good, all capable of anything.

The basis for this thinking is that we are all good people. The idea that we are all good people is the core principle of the religion of humanism, not the religion of Christianity. The Christian Gospel begins with the principle that we are not good people and that all have sinned and fallen short of the glory of God. In humanism, good people don't need a god that is outside of themselves, because they are their own god. Their god is good because their god is themselves, so they must be good. But everywhere we look we see the fallen-ness of mankind. Every day the news is of the fallen-ness of man and the "not goodness" of man. The evidence is overwhelming that man is not good and needs to be redeemed by God. So if man is not good, where does his value come from? Is man valuable at all if he is not good?

The humanists' conclude that the problems in society are a result of good people not knowing their true capacity for being good. In other words, we don't know that we're really good people. If we were more in touch with the reality of how good we are inside, we would be better people. Our problem, it is concluded, is our self-image. Therefore, we have a plethora of seminars, books, lectures, etc., to improve one's self-image, which are founded on the premise that inherently good people do bad things because, for whatever reason, they have bad self-images.

The problem with this approach is that all of the self-image seminars in the world cannot keep us from doing bad things because we are not good people. Bad things don't happen to good people because there are no good people. Years ago there was a book titled Why Do Bad Things Happen To Good People? The question and the book title should be Why Do Bad Things Happen to Bad People? Or more accurately, Why Do Good Things Happen to Bad People? The real amazing grace of God is that any good thing happens to all of us bad people. But now I'm ahead of myself.

The real problem with self-image psychology is that it is hollow and even in some cases counterproductive. Let's say a great motivational speaker comes to the high school and gives a stunning talk on the need for a positive self-image, how good we all are and how, if we just believe in ourselves and realize how good we are, we'll be good citizens of the world. He encourages us to be in touch with the goodness inside ourselves and live accordingly. Everyone is very enthusiastic and excited about the new world that will ensue.

Then that night each person goes home alone and reflects on the day's pep rally for improved self-esteem. As each person lies alone in bed that night, he or she realizes that inside them, there are evil desires and thoughts. Each person wants to do bad things, and the resolutions made during the day have faded into the reality of the night.

Then they consider the premise of the speaker, "We're all good people." This is not consistent with what they know about themselves. They know on an individual basis that they are not good, but they've been told that all people are good inside. They conclude that the "normal" world must be good (everyone says so) but that they are part of the rare breed of humanity that is bad. They see themselves as much worse than their peers, who must be the good people the speaker was talking about. The feelings of loneliness and isolation are intensified, and they sink into despair. They go to bed feeling worse about themselves after the self-image talk then they did before. They know the truth about themselves—that they are not good people—and they are more depressed than ever.

The next day at school, this student begins to find people who are like-minded. He begins to look around and find the other kids who are involved in bad things and who have given up on being good. Being good becomes an impossible task, and as individuals give up on the possibility of being good people, they sink further and further into undesirable activities.

It is into this worldview that the Gospel can speak the most profound truth. We are not good people. We are valuable but we are not good. We need a savior. We need to be rescued from our sin and we cannot rescue ourselves. God has done what we cannot do for ourselves. He has put our sin on the only perfect person—His Son, Jesus—who died for us and has forgiven us of our sin. We can now live life by walking in His spirit, forgiven and cleansed of our sin.

In our Christian culture, we tend to think of the metaphor that we're drowning and need someone to save us. The better metaphor however is to see ourselves as dead on the bottom of the ocean and completely helpless. In this case, we don't need someone to save us. What we need if we're dead is someone to put new life back into us. This is the condition in which God finds us—utterly and hopelessly spiritually dead. He puts the new life into us by His spirit through Christ.

DAN

Dan prayed "the sinner's prayer" because he was convicted of his sexual sin. He was told he was basically a good person, but because of his sins, he would not go to heaven. He was told, "If he would pray a certain prayer and ask Jesus into his life, he would become a Christian and God would forgive him of his sin." He was also told that after he "opened the door, and let Jesus into his life, ᵛhe would have to clean up his life and stop sinning." He tried very hard to live by the rules of the Bible and to control his sexual desires. He thought he was a good person who needed God to help him with his sin. He believed that "God helps those who help themselves," and he was doing his part to be good. How long do you think Dan lasted? Perhaps more importantly, do you think Dan ever really understood the Gospel?

Dan gave up on the Christian faith in a matter of weeks, because he couldn't keep himself good. Then after abandoning any hope of being a good person, his life spun out of control, and he completely indulged in any available sexual activity. He moved out of the social circle he was in before he prayed the prayer, and ended the relationships he had with Christians and made all new friendships with people who shared his propensity for wild living. He was much worse than before he "prayed the prayer." Why?

Dan's problem was that he wasn't good to begin with. Only God is good, and when we equate ourselves with God, we commit the sin that was the root of Adam and Eve's rebellion—wanting to be like God. In so doing, we are trapped in our sin because we assert our equality with God.

Dan's false conversion was built on a false premise. Dan isn't a good person who needed God's help to be better; he is a bad person who needs a Savior. He wasn't good before he "prayed the prayer," and he really wasn't that much better after he "prayed the prayer."

If when Dan "prayed the prayer" he was saved, it is because of the righteousness of Christ, not because of the goodness of Dan. He is not good, but he is God's. And if Dan has truly been saved, then he is as righteous as God, because of Christ's death on the cross.

Second Corinthians 5:21 says, "For He made Him who knew no sin to be sin for us, that we might become the righteousness of God in Him." This means that God made Christ our substitute for sin, and when He looks at us, He sees us as righteous as Himself because of Christ. We're still not inherently good, but because of Christ we are righteous.

14

Since Dan is not a good person, he is not inherently good enough to correct himself. He does not have the inner goodness required to change his bad behavior or desires, and his predicament is hopeless unless a good agent acts upon him. A friend has related the story of a couple who went to Russia to adopt a baby. When they returned home with their new child, they discovered that the baby was ill and was actually turning gray. They took him immediately to the doctor who informed them that the child was one day away from death. The doctor prescribed the proper medication and nutrition and the baby was nursed back to health. Each of us is a day away from death. We need an external agent to act upon us to restore us to life. We need God to act upon us to give us spiritual new life. We need a Savior!

God must act upon Dan to convict him of his sin. (Remember, it is God's job to convict Dan of his sin and draw Dan to Himself, not ours.) It is in fact God's gift to us that He convicts us of our sin. It is part of His love for us that He convicts us of our sin because without the conviction of our sin we cannot throw ourselves completely at His mercy and depend completely upon His Grace for our salvation.

We are in the same boat with Dan, one sinner admitting to another sinner that we're bad people, hopeless, and desperate without the power of God in our lives. Does this sound too extreme? Our condition before a holy God is extreme, and we are absolutely dependent on an extreme savior to save us. On God's side of the ledger, we must put that it is God's job to convict people of their sin and draw people to Himself.

THE ROLE OF CHRISTIAN DISCIPLINE

Even after our conversion, we build elaborate mechanisms to try to reinforce the wrong premise that we are basically good people who only need God to help us be better people (as opposed to bad people who need God to save us). We have built all kinds of systems of discipline and accountability to help us be better Christians, not understanding the fundamental truth that we will struggle with our fallen state until the day Christ eternally calls us to Himself in glory.

There is a great role and need in our lives for the disciplines of the Christian life. We need to be diligent about studying the Bible and spending time in Scripture memory and prayer, but these things do not make us better people. The disciplines of the Christian faith are acts of responsive love in a relationship with a God who has first loved us. They are our joy, not our burden, and when we undertake such activities, we experience His joy in us.

Spiritual discipline and accountability are great aspects of the Christian life, but they must be built on the proper philosophical and theological foundation. When we have spiritual disciplines built on the premise that we are good people who need discipline to keep us good or make us better, we are headed quickly down the road to legalism. Let us remember that legalism is the consistent heresy addressed in the New Testament.

We must also never think that the disciplines of the faith make God love us more or approve of us more. God doesn't love us more because we memorize scripture or love us less if we don't. He doesn't keep a scorecard and measure how many days in a row we have a devotional time, and love

16

us more when we do and less when we don't. God loves us because He loved us, chose us and called us before the foundation of the world, and nothing—nothing—can separate us from His love.

BAD PEOPLE DO GOOD THINGS

You might be wondering then, how it is that any of us, but particularly non-Christians, does good deeds if we are all bad people. The answer is what theologians call "common grace." This means that God has given all people some ability to do good things and that even non-Christian people do good deeds, but it is only because God has allowed them to do so and has acted upon them to produce a good deed or work. This does not mean that any of us are innately good simply because we occasionally do good things. It means that when we do good things, we must recognize that God in His grace has acted upon us to do something good.

We must see ourselves as the bad people we are, who are constantly dependent upon the saving power of Christ in our lives. This is the essence of the Christian life. We are constantly in need of the power of Christ in our lives not only for our salvation but also for our sanctification as well.

SANCTIFICATION

This principle—that we are helpless without Christ—must be applied to our sanctification as well as our salvation. We must understand that it is not we who accomplish the work of sanctification in either our own lives or the lives of those to whom we minister, but God who accomplishes all. Unless God, by the power of His Holy Spirit working in us is the agent of sanctifying change in our lives, we are only moralists, and we may even find ourselves slipping into the most

17

discussed heresy of the New Testament, legalism. The final item on God's side of the ledger is that God is the agent of our sanctification. God is the one who changes us from the inside and makes us conform to the image of His Son.

God's job, therefore, is three key things. First, He convicts us of our sin, second, He draws us to Himself, and third, He sanctifies us.

II. THE EVANGELIST'S JOB

A. COMMUNICATE THE GOSPEL CLEARLY

But what is our responsibility as evangelists in the proclamation of the Gospel? Again, let's turn to the Scripture. We see that we are called to preach the Gospel and make disciples of all nations (Matthew 28:18–20). Therefore, we are called to be proclaimers of the Gospel by the preaching of the Good News. This is different from having the responsibility of drawing people to God by our preaching. Paul tells us in 1 Corinthians 2:1–5 that we are not to use great words or fancy arguments for fear that we might get in the way of the power of Christ. Ours is not the job of convincing people of either their need for Christ or the validity of the Gospel. Our job is only to present the Gospel clearly.

We might debate over what the word "clearly" means, but this will have to be left to the leading of the Holy Spirit in each person's life. We must understand that we are not to be manipulators of other people by the great talks we give— either by our ability to manipulate people with our superlative speaking style, our humor, or by emotional manipulation— hoping to convince some by our own power to make a public profession of faith. This is not our job. Our job is to be communicators of the Gospel, so that as part of the mystery of salvation, God will use our words in the way He wants and bring some to salvation.

By the same token, it would be irresponsible to assume that we can speak gibberish in our proclamation of the Gospel, and God will use it in "effectual calling"—the mystery of the proclaimed Word of God affecting a person's soul. Yes, God can use anything to bring people to salvation, but He entrusts to us with the ministry of reconciliation (1 Corinthians 5) and our responsibility is to be clear communicators of the Gospel. On our side of the ledger, we must clearly communicate the Gospel.

B. Love People

The next issue we want to add to our side of the ledger is to love people. We are all familiar with the great passage of love in 1 Corinthians 13, and we are called above all else to love others. In fact, Paul is so strong on this point that he says that if we have all the other gifts, including the gift of evangelism, but have not love, we are missing the boat. Without love we are no more than making loud noises, and our message is lost in the clatter of the world around us. We must be committed to loving others as Christ has loved us unconditionally, truthfully, and sacrificially if we are to obediently live out our side of the ledger.

We also must understand that it is impossible for us to love others in the way Christ loves them on our own power. We must depend on Christ and His power in us to enable us to love others. The key to being able to love others is to love others as a response to Christ and His love for us. Remember that Christ has said, "He who is forgiven much loves much." If we struggle in loving someone—even our enemies—we need to remember how much we have been forgiven by Christ for our sins, and we will have a fresh perspective on the reason to love others.

This is particularly true when we look at our own role in salvation—that we responded to the prodding of Christ. When we realize that:

1) We are and have been utterly sinful and without ability or merit of our own to come to Christ.

2) That Christ has drawn us to Himself.

3) That Christ has paid the penalty for our sin.

4) That Christ alone is the source of our salvation.

We cannot escape this common link we have with other human beings. Then we cannot help but realize that we are all in the same boat and have no basis upon which to judge others. We must be motivated to love others because:

1) Jesus has first loved us.

2) Jesus has forgiven us.

3) Jesus has commanded us to do so.

C. PRAYER

In this discussion of divine sovereignty and human responsibility, the last issue we will look at is prayer. The Bible implores us to be people of prayer, and in the human responsibility column must appear prayer. Since I will devote the next section to a basic theology of prayer, I will suffice it to say here that we are to be active prayers, because God has commanded us to pray for one another and because Jesus has modeled a life of prayer for us. Again, we do not pray of our own power but as a response to the prompting of the Holy Spirit, lest we find a reason to boast of our own goodness or works. Prayer is our responsibility as Christians in the process of God moving in our lives and in the lives of others. The effects of prayer are God's.

I would also point out that God's work is not dependent upon our prayers. Sometimes we think that great evangelistic accomplishments are a result of our efforts in prayer. But I would remind us that no one prayed for Nineveh and yet God did a great work of repentance among the people of Nineveh using a less than enthused servant, Jonah. We must remember that evangelism is a work of God and that He can use anyone—even us—so that He and He alone gets the glory.

Therefore the three jobs of the evangelist are:

1) Proclaim the Gospel clearly.

2) Love people.

3) Pray for people.

III. MAN'S JOB

Now that we have discussed God's job (drawing people to Himself, convicting people of their sin, and sanctifying us) and the evangelist's job (loving people, praying for them, and communicating the Gospel clearly), what is man's responsibility? I want to begin with the definition of the word "responsibility" found in Steve Covey's book The Seven Habits of Highly Effective People. He says, "Responsibility [is] the ability to choose your response."[vi]

This is what our "human responsibility" means: the ability God has given us to respond to Him after He has moved first in all areas of our lives.

If it is God who is responsible for drawing us to Him, then what is the responsibility of man in the process of conversion? The first thing we must understand is that our job (responsibility) is to respond to God's calling. As the recipients of God's effective calling, our job is to respond to that call by repenting of our sin, turning from our sin, and committing our lives to following Him. While even these acts cannot occur without the power of God in our life, it is our responsibility to act on the prompting of God and respond to Him.

Love always demands a response. As God has loved us in the sending and giving of His Son, we must respond to that love. Most of us have had the experience of having someone tell us they love us. Sometimes we feel the same emotion and we tell the person we love them also. Sometimes, however, we do not share that feeling and we have to say, "But I don't feel the same way about you." At other times we might not have a particular emotion at all about the person.

As we can respond to human love in three ways, so can we also respond to the love of Christ in three ways: 1) by rejecting the love of Christ, 2) by being indifferent to that love, or 3) by loving God and trusting Him with our lives. When we respond to the love of God by confessing Christ as Lord and believing in our hearts that God raised Him from the dead, we become Christians (Romans 10:9).

So let's return to our chart. In its most basic form, it would look like this:

GOD'S JOB	THE EVANGELIST'S JOB	MAN'S JOB
1. CONVICT PEOPLE OF SIN.	1. LOVE PEOPLE.	1. RESPOND.
2. DRAW PEOPLE TO HIMSELF.	2. PRAY FOR PEOPLE.	
3. SANCTIFY PEOPLE.	3. PRESENT THE GOSPEL CLEARLY.	

This list may seem simplistic as you look at it here, but consider how we have too often reversed the list and taken upon ourselves the things that are God's responsibility. We have wanted to convict people of their sin, draw them to God, and, once converted, to make them holy people.

At the same time, we want God to love people (we casually say, "God loves you" which of course He does, but that does not negate our responsibility), we want God to be concerned for people ("God will take care of you"), and we want God to make the message clear ("It really doesn't matter what I say; the Holy Spirit will get through"). Now it's not that God doesn't love people; He loves people more than we ever could. It's not that God isn't concerned for people; He is more concerned than we will ever be. And it's not that the Holy Spirit won't get his message through; He even used Jonah to prove that point. The point here is that God has given us the ministry of reconciliation (1 Corinthians 5) and allowed us the privilege of prayer, love, and communication. We must do all of this to the best of the ability God has given us. That is our responsibility.

A BRIEF THEOLOGY OF PRAYER

We begin with a simple definition of prayer, "conversation with God." Prayer in its essence is man communicating with God through his spirit, and God communicating to man through His Spirit. But prayer is also an act of God in us. Paul tells us in Romans 8:26–27 that we do not even know how to pray as we ought, so God's Spirit intercedes for us with our spirit to prod us and to lead us and to bring our requests before the throne of the Lord.

In Larry Crabb's excellent book, Inside Out, he deals with the problem of a demanding spirit in each of us. He tells us that we have substituted a humble attitude toward God for a demanding spirit toward God. This attitude is founded on the flawed principle that God owes us certain things and we have certain rights to live the good life.

In 1 Samuel 8, we read about the appointment of Saul to be king of Israel. You will remember that the nation of Israel was not a monarchy governed by kings but rather a nation governed by prophets that the Lord Himself appointed and spoke through. At this time in Israel's history, the Prophet Samuel was the Prophet in charge, and the people came to him and demanded that they be given a king so they could be like the other nations. They looked around the world and saw that other nations had kings, and they wanted to be like the other nations, so they went to Samuel and demanded that God give them a king. Samuel was grieved but God's response to Samuel was that the people had not rejected Samuel but had rejected Him (God) as their king (v. 7–8). It is worth noting that it was anticipated that Israel would have a king (Gen. 49:10, Num. 24:7, 17-19, and Deut 17:14-20) but the question was one of timing. They wanted a king in their timing—not God's.

We see this attitude today. We look around at our neighbors and our friends, we see what they have, and we become bitter and angry with God that He has not provided for us in the same way He has provided for others. We see people

24

who have nicer homes, faster cars, or bigger mini-vans than we have. We see people whose children are better looking, get better grades, or are better behaved than our own children are. We see people who are more fulfilled in their vocations than we are or who take better vacations than we do. We see those who have skyboxes at the stadium or fly first class when we're back in coach and we want what they have. But our demanding is not limited to material possessions. We demand good health, loving and supportive families, and caring relationships. We look around at those who live beside us and we want to be like them, and we demand that God give us what others have.

We believe that if God is all powerful and He loves us, then He should share some of that power with us and send some of His blessings our way. In some skewed way, we believe we have a "right" to material and spiritual happiness. In recent years there has been a tremendous rise in the "health and wealth" version of the Gospel. The idea is propagated that King David and King Solomon were rich, and if we obey God and live for Him, we should be just as rich. Perhaps the low point of this kind of thinking is in the idea that if we pray a certain prayer from the Old Testament, God will increase our kingdom. The problem with all of this is it's not the Gospel!

The Gospel is not about what God owes us, it is about our utter sinfulness and the fact that we deserve nothing but judgment and death from God, but instead He has given us forgiveness and life. We have no right to demand anything of God. We are only to respond to Him and His goodness and mercy upon us by relinquishing our lives to Him in praise for His overwhelming love for us. While we were yet sinners, Christ died for us and brought us into the presence of the almighty, living God. This and this alone is the Gospel, and we must embrace nothing less.

So what does this have to do with prayer? When the people of Israel demanded a king, the shocking news is that God gave them what they demanded. God told Samuel that the people had not rejected Samuel but had rejected Him (God) from being king over them; so He gave them what they wanted and appointed the disastrous Saul as king over Israel. This should scare the stew out of all of us. The idea that God may give us the things that we demand, even if it's not His best, should drive us to our knees in desperate repentance (in fact, it was after the disastrous Saul that God appointed his own servant David. Perhaps God allowed the disaster under Saul to prepare the people to appreciate the appointment of David). We may actually be praying demanding prayers and receiving answers to our demanding prayers that are not the best for us. And to make things worse, we will be deceived into thinking we're spiritual because God is answering our prayers.

This may be startling news for many of us. We have been taught to pray demanding prayers. We even believe that the more we demand, the more faith we are displaying and the more spiritual we are, when in fact the opposite may be true. As you think about this, you find yourself not even knowing how to pray. Fortunately, Jesus has given us great models of prayer. You will remember that He taught us how to pray in the Sermon on the Mount (the Lord's Prayer found in Matthew 6:5–15 and Luke 11:1–4) and then again demonstrates the practice of prayer in the Garden of Gethsemane.

In the Sermon on the Mount, Jesus tells us there are to be a few important elements in our prayers. First, we are to acknowledge that God is our Father and that He is supreme over all of heaven and earth. Second, we are to understand that we are to desire God's will be done on earth, the same way it is accomplished in heaven. Third, we are to remember our sin and to remember that God is the source of our forgiveness. We must rely on Him to forgive us, and then we will be motivated to forgive others. Fourth, we must remember that it is God who protects us from evil and delivers us from sin. Lastly, we must acknowledge that God is the one who is supreme over all. The prayer of Jesus is one in which the sovereignty of God is submitted to, and one in which we desire for His kingdom to come, not ours to be increased.

You will notice in this model of prayer that there is nothing even remotely similar to a demanding spirit. We are not told to demand anything, only to rely upon God for the sum of our existence. We are specifically told to ask for God's will to be done, and nowhere are we asked to demand that our will be done. We cannot justify a demanding spirit in prayer based upon the model of prayer given to us by Jesus. We can only come to God in prayer in a state of humble obedience, knowing the tremendous privilege of being able to communicate with the God of the universe.

Lest we think that this is simply a nice outline of prayer given to us by Jesus, we are also given the application of this principle of prayer in the most difficult time in Jesus's life. At the point in His life when Jesus knew He was going to be betrayed, would soon be abandoned by his friends, tortured, and crucified in an excruciatingly painful death, He modeled prayer to us. You will remember that on that night in the Garden of Gethsemane Jesus prayed intensely that the cup would pass from him, but nevertheless, not His will but God's will be done.

Here we have the key to the kind of prayers we are to pray. Jesus does not hold back his emotions from His Father. In fact, He pours out the deepest and most intense emotions of His life to the Lord and begs for the cup to pass from Him. He knows the pain and the death that awaits Him. He was fully human and fully God and the human part of Him wanted the cup of death to pass from Him. He was also able to give over the decision to the Father and prayed that while His emotion and desire was to not go to the cross, He would relinquish His own will to that of the Father. These are the key elements of prayer.

We are to express both of these elements in our prayers. We are to pour out our deepest emotions, needs, wants and desires upon the Lord. We are also to surrender our own will to the will of the Lord, acknowledging that He is the one in control of our lives and that we must surrender our lives to Him.

But what about Luke 18? Isn't that a model of demanding prayer? Luke 18:1-8 is the parable of the demanding widow. Let me give you a principle for studying the Bible as we look at this passage. If there is a verse in a section of Scripture that doesn't seem to belong or doesn't seem to make sense in the context of the rest of the passage, then that verse is probably the key to re-understanding the passage. Such is the case with Luke 18.

You will notice that Jesus teaches that the widow has no right to come to the unrighteous judge. Nonetheless, after she has harassed him, he gives into her demands in order to stop her from annoying him. Jesus says that so much more will God give to us whom He loves. This is a statement of fact. It teaches us about the nature of God, about how much He loves His children, and that He is indeed so powerful that He is able to grant the wishes of His children.

But have you noticed verse 8? It is the verse that doesn't seem to make sense. Verse 8 says, "Nevertheless, when the Son of Man comes will He find faith on earth?" What does this mean? I believe that in the context of what we have already seen about prayer, Jesus is saying that, yes, God is able and will indeed answer demanding prayers—just as He did with the Israelites in giving them King Saul—but what He wants from His people is faith. He wants His people to have faith that He (God) is for them ("If God is for us who can be against us?") and will take care of them ("all things work together for good for those who love God and are called according to His purpose"), and will look out for them without them demanding their will of Him.

In the Greek the word, πιστευω is used for "faith," "trust," and "believe." We could see this verse, as "Nevertheless when the Son of Man comes will He find trust on earth?" Jesus is asking us if we will trust God in our prayers rather than have a demanding spirit. He wants us to have a spirit of humble trust in and obedience to God. We must focus our prayers on God, and while pouring out our emotions, desires, and needs to the Lord (after all, He already knows them), we must relinquish our will to His and trust Him with our lives. This is great news for us, and we can rejoice in knowing that the things that trouble us the most are in the hands of the One who created the universe and is concerned for every hair on our heads.

What then does this mean about the way we pray in our ministry? How should we pray for people to come to Christ or for more laborers to work with us, or supporters to give money? As I look back on my years of ministry, I see that for many years I prayed demanding prayers about the various aspects of the ministry. When prayers were answered, I thought God was really blessing my demanding prayers. The harder I prayed, the more I thought God blessed—as if God's will for other people's eternal destiny was determined by the intensity of my prayers.

For example, there were kids for whom I was very burdened and cared deeply about their eternal destiny. In the past, I might have prayed for this kid in a demanding way to the Lord. I might have said, "Lord, make this kid come to Club. You know he needs to hear about You, and he needs to be at Club to hear about You, and I just pray that You will make him come. I just want to pray for this name over and over—Mike, Mike, Mike, and ask again and again that you will make him come to Club, go to camp, and stand up at the say-so. I know that you will answer my prayer if I continue to bring this name before You, so I'll ask you again to bring Mike to Club and to move in his spirit to want to be there and to put him on the bus for camp and make him open the door of his life to You and stand up at the say-so." I would repeat this prayer or some form of it over and over every day, and when Mike came to Club, I would check him off the list and begin praying harder that he would go to camp.

But it was a demanding prayer. It had at its root a false premise that I could manipulate the will of God; and it was wrong. Today I pray,

Lord, You know how much I care about Mike. I know You've put him on my heart, and I am deeply grieved in my spirit about the pain in his life and how much he needs You. I pray that You would touch his life and work in his spirit. I pray that You would convict him of his sin and draw him to You. I ask that You give me the strength and courage to love him and to care about him in the way You want me to. Nevertheless Lord, not my will, but Your will be done.

We can experience the joy of prayer and of intimate fellowship with the Lord when we let go of our demanding prayers and pour out our most intimate thoughts to the Lord and trust Him for His will to be done. Then the joy of answered prayer comes from knowing that the God of the universe has used even us to be part of accomplishing His will.

BIBLICAL TEXTS

Now that we've discussed some theological foundations for our ministry, we will look at some verses, which provide a foundation for the specific ministry of evangelism. These verses are grouped together to provide a firm base of Scripture to draw from. In this way we can first look at the Biblical text before drawing from it.

Matthew 28:19: "Go therefore and make disciples of all nations, baptizing them in the name of the Father and of the Son and of the Holy Spirit..." This command of Jesus is to make disciples not just converts. Our ministry must be disciple oriented.

Mark 6:7: "And he called to Him the twelve, and began to send them out two by two, and gave them authority over the unclean spirits." Jesus sent his disciples out, gave them a significant other to be in partnership with, and gave them the ministry of having authority over the unclean spirits.

John 10:14: "I am the good shepherd; I know my own and my own know me, as the Father knows me and I know the Father; and I lay down my life for the sheep." The model Jesus gives us is one of laying down His life for His sheep, and we are to do the same.

John 13:34–35: "A new commandment I give to you that you love one another; even as I have loved you, that you also love one another. By this all men will know that you are my disciples, if you have love for one another." We are commanded as disciples of Christ to love others with our lives. Our disciples must also love others with their lives.

John 15:13: "Greater love has no man than this, that a man lay down his life for his friends." Jesus shows us what real love means by laying down His life for us and sacrificing Himself on the cross.

John 15:16: "You did not choose me, but I chose you and appointed you that you should go and bear fruit and that your fruit should abide..." Jesus says His purpose for us is (1) that we bear fruit ourselves and (2) that our fruit abides in Him. This must be the purpose of our ministry.

Ephesians 4:11–13: "It was He who gave some to be apostles, some to be prophets, some to be evangelists, and some to be pastors and teachers, to prepare God's people for works of service, so that the body of Christ may be built up until we all reach unity in the faith and in the knowledge of the

Son of God and become mature, attaining to the whole measure of the fullness of Christ." We are to grow together with our various gifts for works of service to others. The idea of Christians existing only for themselves is not a New Testament concept.

Colossians 1:28: "Him we proclaim, warning every man and teaching every man in all wisdom, that we may present every man mature in Christ." Paul's goal was to present every man mature in Christ. There was no thought of conversions without discipleship.

1 Thessalonians 2:8: "So, being affectionately desirous of you, we were ready to share with you not only the Gospel of God but also our own selves, because you had become very dear to us." True discipleship involves not only the proclamation of the Gospel but also the sharing of our lives with those to whom we are ministering. Our ministry must reflect this type of discipleship.

1 Timothy 2:3–4: "This is good, and it is acceptable in the sight of God our Savior, who desires all men to be saved and to come to the knowledge of the truth." The full knowledge of truth is the goal of our ministry.

2 Timothy 2:2: "And what you have heard from me before many witnesses entrust to faithful men who will be able to teach others also." We are to pass on what God has given to us to others who are faithful in order that they will be able to teach others also. The idea of reproducing ourselves is the New Testament model.

c✒Chapter Two✒

Philosophical Basis

From the preceding verses, three major points of philosophy may be drawn.

The first principle is that Jesus's command was to go to the whole world (1 Timothy 2:3–4). We must possess a burning urgency to reach all people. This drives us not to settle for small groups of people. Jesus had compassion for the crowds and multitudes and ministered to them. We must see our aim as one of reaching an entire high school and not limit ourselves to a select few. This may seem to be contradictory to the following points on discipleship, but as I will explain, God's model of reproducing reproducers is a vision for reaching all people that merely requires patience and faith.

The second principle is that our ministry must be relational. It is life upon life; it is one person expending his life for the lives of others. Paul says in 2 Corinthians 12:15, "I

34

will most gladly spend and be spent for your souls." In our culture today, we are so self-consumed that the idea of our being "spent" for the soul of another is completely foreign to us. We subtly adopt the world's view that we are to look out for number one, which is ourselves. That view is contrary to the model and teaching of Jesus. The model of Jesus is that He lays down his life for us (John 10:17, 15:13).

The essence of ministry is that Christians, in obedience to Christ, give of themselves—their time, their resources, their emotions, and their lives—to other people in order that they may come to know Jesus and follow Him.

Jesus not only talked about investing His life into others, He spent His entire public ministry modeling it. Jesus invested in twelve men and modeled for us what true relational ministry and leadership looks like. Jesus's death and resurrection could have been accomplished without the twelve disciples, yet He spent the public part of His ministry making twelve men his best friends. Jesus did not invest His life in twelve men because it was necessary for our salvation or sanctification. The reason He made this investment was to give us a model of ministry. His life was one of investing Himself strategically in a few people, and I believe He did it to serve as a model to us forever.

The following are a few examples of relational ministry beyond the confines of what we might imagine.

One day my wife got a call from one of our former Campaigner kids who had also been one of her dearest friends and disciples. This young woman was really struggling at college with some family problems and life issues. It became apparent that a phone conversation was not going to be enough. Without hesitation, we decided that my wife should drive to Philadelphia, get on the train, and spend a couple of days with this girl. Yes, there were other responsibilities in the area. There were meetings she would miss and tasks that she needed to perform, but this girl needed her, and the principle that people are more important than program took precedence. Debbie said, "The weekend wasn't one of all deep conversations, prayer and solving problems. A lot of the weekend involved playing cards, sharing meals, and going for silent walks. The important thing was that at this critical juncture of this girl's life, I just went to 'be with her' because I loved her and wanted to be there with and for her."

When another Campaigner kid/disciple went off to college, we continued to be in touch. I was able to arrange most of my flights to go through the hub city where he went to college and, for a few extra dollars, stay over an extra night to see him. On one of those occasions when I stopped for the weekend, it was, in God's providence, a critical time in his life. We spent forty-eight hours just sitting and talking about life and what it means to be God's people. We only left his room for meals. That weekend was a turning point for both of us, as we developed an even deeper friendship.

We must understand that our call to be missionaries means being with people, listening to them, caring about them, sharing with them, and giving of ourselves to them. It is not a program; it is a relationship. We must be relational people in order to have a relational ministry.

I asked Mike Sambrook, one of the Canadian staff members while I was Ontario Director, to write the following story for inclusion in this book because it is a wonderful example of caring for kids and the impact it has. Here in Mike's words is that story.

"The night before leaving for Disney World with sixty kids on our annual Young Life camp trip, I was hanging out with two Campaigner guys. We were picking up some last-minute items for the trip while chatting about our objectives for this trip and praying for the guys' friends who would join us.

Unfortunately, their best friend Matt, who had met Christ on the same trip the previous year, was not able to join us this time. Matt's parents would not let him attend this year, and he had been depressed for weeks. As we drove around town, we found out that Matt was at a party hosted by a friend of his named Brad. Brad was known to host the biggest parties with a lot of drugs and alcohol.

The Campaigner guys were concerned, so we drove to Brad's house to check on Matt and see if we might 'rescue' him from himself. As we pulled into the driveway, I could see Brad sitting in the window of his bedroom. 'Hey, Mike', he shouted down, 'are you here for Matt?' I said yes. 'He's not doing to well,' Brad replied, 'he's had a lot to drink.'

"I sent the guys in to retrieve Matt while I chatted with Brad from the driveway below. There were about fifty kids in and around the house, most of whom I knew by name. Brad came down from the window and met me in the driveway; about a dozen others joined him. We sat on the hood of my car for what seemed like an eternity as Joel and Dan attempted to retrieve Matt—it turned out he had locked himself in the bathroom out of shame. The guys returned to the car unsuccessful in their mission. I reminded the guys of their commitment to Matt and challenged them that a bathroom door should be no match for a couple of high school rugby players and sent them back into Brad's house.

"This is when the conversation became fantastic! Brad recognized the relational intensity of the moment: the fact that we had come to his party to rescue our friend, our commitment to not let a locked door stop us, and the fact that a 'youth leader' would come to a drunken party, his party, for a friend. 'Are you angry with Matt,' Brad asked.

"'I'm disappointed in him, Brad,' I replied. ' Matt is my friend, and I know this is not what he wants to do with his life.'

"'Are you disappointed in me?' asked Brad. This was an amazing question, one that has stuck with me to this day. You see, Brad understood the disappointment was rooted in love.

"'No, I'm not disappointed with you Brad.'

"'Why not,' said Brad, 'Why won't you be disappointed with me?'

"Now it became great. Brad was really asking, "Why won't you love me like you love Matt?' He desperately desired a friend who would come to rescue him. He knew that he too was not living the life he really wanted, and he desperately wanted someone to love him, to be disappointed in him, like Joel, Dan, and I were with Matt.

"What followed was a twenty-minute conversation about friendship, accountability, judgment, and grace. Finally, the guys returned with an ashamed Matt, and we piled into my car to get some coffee and sober Matt up. Brad and about seven of his friends who had listened intently to the entire conversation asked if they could join us and attempted to pile into the car as well. I had to remind Brad this was his house and that he might need to get some control of the party before it was ruined.

"I tell this story often, and I believe it to be definitive of the Gospel. We live relationally with those who are crying out, 'Why won't you love me?' We have been given the ministry of reconciliation; a call to retrieve a broken person from a party they were not meant for. When we engage in these deep loving relationships, those around us will know we are Christ's disciples because of this love we have for one another. Deep relationships between followers of Christ are mysterious to the unbeliever because they are spiritual. I believe God designed it this way, and I believe it is a significant aspect of the mission to which we were called—to make disciples."

The third principle God calls us to in ministry is that of discipleship (Matthew 28:19). Many of our problems in ministry stem from our inability to grasp this important tenet. Jesus does not charge us to go and make converts. He tells us to make disciples. My study of the New Testament reveals no example where conversion without discipleship was affirmed.

Conversely, discipleship without a heart for lost people would not be discipleship. The two concepts must go together and in my view are inseparable. Therefore the fourth principle is that we must be passionate about evangelism. Evangelism and Discipleship must coexist as one entity in the life of the believer. To describe this interconnecting relationship between discipleship and evangelism, we will use my newly created word "disciplevangelism."

As evangelicals, we have traditionally been so focused on the masses hearing the Gospel that we have all too often discarded the discipleship part of our ministry. We build relationships with kids so that we can win the right to proclaim the message of the Gospel to them. After proclaiming the Gospel, we move on to other relationships in order to reach more kids. We develop a "passing parade" mentality that looks at each generation of high school kids as a float in a parade that passes by our ministry. We hit them with the Gospel, and as they move on, we hit the next float. This, of course, is not the biblical model.

Perhaps we believe that this is the most efficient model, or we are afraid that some will not be reached if we don't cast the widest net. If we take the model of Jesus seriously, then we must let go of our fears that some will not be reached and focus our attention on building disciples. In the long run, building disciples who will reach others is the best way to reach the masses, but it requires patience and trust that God's model for us will be honored by Him.

This approach requires patience that the ministry will happen over a longer period of time than we may want. We need to think in terms of impacting generations and not just immediate results. It has been said that we tend to overestimate what we can accomplish in five years and underestimate what God can accomplish in a lifetime. It requires faith and trust to believe God that His way is best. The great faith chapter of Hebrews 11 is about people who trusted that God's way was best and waited upon God for His timing. We must be those kinds of people.

In summary, the philosophical basis can be stated as three things:

1. MASS

2. RELATIONAL

3. DISCIPLEVANGELISM

These three tenets must be held together as one philosophical base. We cannot sacrifice one principle for another. The three must be interwoven like a strong rope, each strand equally important to the total strength of the rope. Another way to view this would be the box following illustration.

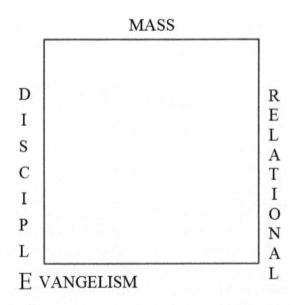

As we examine our ministry, we want to make sure that what we do fits inside the box. Inside the box there is great individuality and creativity. Each person's ministry will be unique to that person's gifts and personality, but it must fall within the parameters of the box. An architect friend told me that the highest forms of creativity happen inside a given set of parameters. We tend to think that real creativity happens outside the box, but in fact it requires more creativity to create something beautiful inside the box. Now we are ready to build our function, the macro ways in which our ministry will operate.

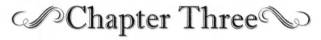

Chapter Three

FUNCTION

The function of our ministry could also be referred to as our purpose. It is that which our ministry is intended to accomplish. The function of a car is to provide transportation. The function of a building is to provide shelter. The function of a restaurant is to make money (selling food is the form). To determine the function of our ministry, we need to draw on what we believe Biblical and philosophically about ministry.

First, we will draw on the concept of MASS. Our function will include ways for our ministry to reach lots of kids. We know that our role is to proclaim Christ to the masses so it might be helpful for us to put some numbers on the words "large" and "small." My belief is that you only begin to impact a high school when you are engaging at least 10 percent of the kids in a given school; so less than 10 percent is small. Our strategy and forms will need to be designed to reach and attract large numbers of kids.

Next, let's consider how the philosophy of RELATIONAL becomes a function. Our function will need to involve opportunities for lives to touch other lives and for our disciples and us to invest ourselves in others. Whatever we do will involve the lives of Christians being invested in the lives of others. We must guard against the temptation of being drawn into gimmicks of any sort in order to attract the mass of kids. These gimmicks take the place of relationships and subvert the relational approach.

People today are highly attuned to schemes that are designed to sell them something. We have all heard of the many scams out there that offer us a deal on something that is too good to be true. We are a nation of savvy shoppers who are particularly sensitive to the "bait and switch" tactic of attracting us to a product with one enticement and then sneaking in an alternate agenda once we've signed on. In this way, we've become a culture of cynics, not trusting anyone to honestly represent what he or she is selling.

We cannot succumb to this temptation. We are not "selling" Jesus with mass marketing, slick advertisements, and polished slogans. We are beggars telling other beggars where to find food, and we do so relationally. While we are committed to telling lots of people about the love of Christ, we cannot sacrifice the principle of relationships on the altar of mass outreach. These principles must coexist and cannot be at cross-purposes. Events and gimmicks, designed to draw kids to a program or event without the involvement of a person will be rejected outright. That type of strategy subverts the philosophy of "life upon life" as it attempts to attract kids to a program or event and not a person.

When I first moved to Bethlehem, Pennsylvania, I was sitting in my office one day and the phone rang. The voice on the other end of the line said, "This is so-and-so from the ice cream store and I'm calling to take your ice cream order."

I said, "But I didn't order any ice cream."

The salesperson said, "Oh, every year at this time I call for your order for the banana split. You always make the one hundred foot long banana split to get kids to come to your event."

"I'm sorry," I replied, "that was the person whose place I've just taken, and we won't be doing that anymore."

I don't want kids attracted to us because of banana splits. I want them attracted to us because of Christ. This is the core thesis of this book, and I have put together the following list to give concrete reasons why the "gimmick" and "event" mentality are counterproductive to quality ministry.

Eight Reasons Why Gimmicks and Events Are Counterproductive to Quality Ministry

1. The Scripture warns against it. In 2 Corinthians 2:17, Paul says, "For we are not, like so many, peddlers of God's Word; but as men of sincerity, as commissioned by God in the sight of God we speak in Christ." The Christian faith must not be sold to the world like used cars on the lot of the church. We must be real people relating to real people with the love of the God of the universe in our hearts, minds, souls, and strength.

2. The attraction of our work should not be our ability to build the greatest banana split. Kids should be attracted to us because they see Jesus in a life that has been invested in theirs.

3. A kid who gets involved because of a banana split (or any other gimmick) will see that gimmick as the model for ministry. He will spend his entire life waiting for someone else to put on the next big event to bring others to Christ and will be robbed of the joy of Christ working through him. Kids will reason that since they got involved via a gimmick, everyone else will be won by a gimmick. Thus the quest begins for the bigger and better gimmick and the relational touch of life upon life is lost. One volunteer leader wanted to raffle off a car each week in order to get more kids at Club. Where will the gimmicks end?

4. I believe the gimmick mentality is part of the reason our kids seem to struggle in adjusting well to college fellowships, which are generally not "banana split" focused. Our kids go to college expecting to be entertained by the

Christian organizations there in the same way there were entertained in high school. Other Christian groups that do not cater to the gimmick-oriented mentality turn them off. The poor model of ministry they were exposed to in high school has cast the die for failure.

5. Gimmicks rob Campaigner kids of experiencing the joy of relational ministry. When they see their classmates coming to Club, camp, and Christ without their involvement, they begin to think that they are an unnecessary part of God's plan for the world. One staff person who heard the principle of "kid ownership" enlisted kids in helping him pick out the costumes and sets for the "show" he put on each week at Club. He missed the point entirely. Props and costumes aren't the ministry of the God of the universe; lives invested in others are.

6. Gimmicks communicate to Campaigner kids that they are untrustworthy in handling the Gospel. Leaders communicate their priorities by where they invest their time. If their time is spent setting up the next gimmick or event, Campaigners will soon realize that the gimmick is more important than spending time with them. Campaigner kids will surely feel that they are not responsible for the significant things of God. My guess is that this is at the root of the resentment many leaders have for their Campaigner kids and vice versa. The leaders do not see the Campaigner kids as partners, but rather as annoyances they must tolerate. The situation compounds itself, and the kids become more alienated and problematic, driving the leader to greater and greater frustration.

7. Gimmicks are short run in their effect. Kids will only come to anything that is the latest and slickest thing on the market for a short period of time before they realize that it's not as good as video games, social media, or whatever else they can get from the world. How many times can the leader shave his head? Competing with the world is the place all gimmicks will ultimately lead.

8. Lastly, I believe that gimmicks/events are exhausting to leaders. Leaders can get burned out trying to top each previous week's gimmick. Soon they become frustrated and discouraged by Club and drop out. We kill some of our best leaders and staff by demanding they come up with a new gimmick each week to attract disinterested kids. One leader told me, "I did the giant pig roast on the beach and we had a hundred kids come. I turned to my wife afterward and said, 'I'm done. That's the biggest event I can do. There has to be another way.'" There is another way. No more gimmicks!

If given the opportunity to say one thing to all in youth ministry, it would be for them to completely forget any and all gimmicks. In my twenty years of Young Life ministry, we have never used any type of gimmick. Never. Not once. We found that quality ministry was better without them.

Here are two scenarios, one with gimmicks and one without.

A gimmick-oriented Club will start large the night of the gimmick and decline each week. You do the big "banana split" in late September, and you have one hundred kids come to your event. The next week you have ninety kids at Club. The next week you have seventy. By the end of October, you have thirty, and by Thanksgiving you have stopped having Club all together. You start up again in February with another big event. By April 1, you are done–Club is back to less than thirty kids and you close it down. You have been selling camp the whole time, so maybe you'll make your camp quota and take twenty-five or thirty kids to camp. This is negative momentum. Just when you want Club to be getting larger—because the talks are getting deeper and it is getting closer to camp—the Club is getting smaller.

So instead of that scenario, you decide to do a gimmick every week and try to keep kids coming because you are doing something "special" every week. The same outcome will happen. Kids will get bored of the gimmicks and see them for what they are—a trick to keep them coming—and bail out of your Club.

On the other hand, a non-gimmick Club will "snowball" each week, causing positive momentum; and it will have a net total greater impact. The Club without a "banana split" will start at thirty kids in mid-September, grow each week, and by the end of October, be hitting fifty kids. By Thanksgiving you will have close to seventy kids each week. By March you will have a consistent seventy with a solid core of kids who go to camp. Let's say that the number of kids who go to camp is the same as in the previous scenario—twenty-five to thirty. But these kids have been in Club all year. They have heard the entire talk sequence. They have been engaging with you and your Campaigners all year. They are prepared to hear the Gospel. They are ready to respond to the Gospel. You have built relationships with them and they are ready to give their lives to Christ.

In business this is called "permission marketing." It means that the "customer" has given you permission to market your product to them. This happens every time you give your email address to a company. You give them permission to send you their marketing material. When you have a club of substance and the kids who go to camp are the ones who have been coming to club all year, then, when they go to camp they are giving you permission to talk to them about Christ. They aren't going because of the video or the para-sail. They are going because they want to be with the Christians who have been investing in them all year.

When I was in Canada there was some thinking that a kid needed to go to camp at least three times before they responded to Christ because Canada was a post Christian country and these kids had not been exposed to Christianity at home. That was true, Canada is a post Christian country, and very few of the kids we worked with came from Christian homes. But the more important factor was that they were not exposed to club each week and were not hearing the Gospel each week at club before they went to camp.

When we moved to a club model in Ontario we saw kids respond to Christ on their first camp trip because they had been in club all year leading up to the camp trip and knew what they were getting in to when they went to camp.

Additionally, when those kids come back from camp, they are ready to take the Club to the next level. In year two, the Club starts in September at fifty kids, is at seventy by the end of October, and now flirts with one hundred kids by Thanksgiving. In the spring you are having consistent Clubs of around one hundred, and now you are taking forty to fifty kids to camp. The next year the momentum continues. This is a far better strategy than continuing to come up with a new gimmick every week to keep kids coming to your event. This is in fact the strategy that I saw work in Baltimore, Bethlehem, St. Louis, and Canada.

DISCIPLEVANGELISM

Finally, let's turn our attention to the concept of "Disciplevangelism." Our function here means that the goal of our work is to build men and women who will not only begin a relationship with Jesus Christ but will also go on in that relationship to maturity. Whatever we do involves the ultimate proclamation of the Gospel and the drawing of Christian kids to a deeper personal walk. We must realize that this is not an either/or proposition (either proclamation or nurture) but both. We must design our forms (primarily contacts, Club, and camp) to enable Christian kids to experience Christ deeply, as well as to proclaim Christ to non-Christian kids. It is discipleship and evangelism integrated together into one life. We must realize that the message Jesus preached to his disciples was one of an entire life change, and that is the message we must proclaim to kids.

THE WHOLE BALL OF WAX

Therefore the basic tenet to be held is that as Christian kids (or any other Christians for that matter) trust and obey Christ by expending themselves in His service for others, they experience the power of Christ deeply in their own lives and grow in their maturity in Christ. This is the underlying principle of everything in this book.

As Christians stretch themselves for others and go beyond their comfort zones, Jesus meets them in a miraculous way. Others respond to Christ as they see Him in a life lived before them. Christian kids then experience the spiritual dynamic often only realized by adult leaders in this process of risking themselves for their friends and standing up for their faith.

A Campaigner kid invites a teammate from the football team to come to Young Life. He is risking his reputation to do so, and he is a little anxious about doing it. He has prayed for courage and finally taken the risk and invited his friend. The friend says "Maybe." Other guys on the team hear of it and start to make fun of the Campaigner kid. They ridicule him for his faith. He experiences a little persecution for his faith. That persecution drives him deeper into his faith and enables him to grow in his faith. He becomes a persecuted witness like New Testament believers before him and his faith deepens. He prays more, and the Scripture comes alive for him. He is growing as a Christian, and he is modeling the faith to others. He is ready to ask his friend again because he is growing in faith.

Additionally, good models are created. As kids see other kids give of themselves for them, they see how to give of themselves to others. This model will last the rest of their lives and will make them lights in any darkness, whether it is in high school, college, within their families, or in the workplace.

The growing Christian life can be compared to our physical bodies. If we simply take in food without expending some energy in the form of exercise, then we only become fat and lethargic. Unfortunately, this is the state of many Christians. They are getting fat, because of only taking in spiritual milk, and lethargic, because of no real exercise of their faith. If all we do is sit and listen to a Bible study, pray for our own needs, and demand that the church entertain us, then we are like a person who only eats but never exercises.

For example, one may do a year's worth of Bible studies on what it means to suffer as a Christian and the great benefits that suffering produces. If we never actually suffer for our faith, however, we will never really understand how God uses suffering to teach us obedience (Hebrews 5:8). On the other hand, if we grow not only in the intake of spiritual things but also in the exercising of our faith, we will grow into more significant work in the body of Christ because we have really grown in our relationship with Christ.

Take any other activity in our lives. You don't become a better baseball player by watching it on TV—you have to actually go out and play the game. You don't become a better pianist by listening to someone else play the piano—you have to sit at the keyboard yourself and learn to play. It's worth noting that watching the pros play is helpful to your growth, but only if you are also playing yourself. So it is with the Christian faith. You don't become a disciple by watching other disciples, you have to "walk the walk" yourself, and then the model of other disciples is extremely helpful.

The goal is to make disciples not converts, and discipleship requires exercise. You don't make disciples by reproducing kids who are looking for the next event to entertain them. You produce disciples by enabling Christians to experience the reality of Christ in their lives. And when you do, no one can tell them that God isn't real. No college professor, no family member, no fraternity, no one. They know from firsthand experience that the God of the universe has met them in a unique and powerful way and that can never change.

Now we are prepared to look at the forms that will facilitate the function, philosophical basis, and Biblical foundation for ministry. The five forms we will look at are: Campaigners, Contacts, Club, Camp, and Alumni.

Chapter Four

Campaigners

THE GATHERING TOGETHER OF CHRISTIANS

We begin by considering what is referred to in Young Life as Campaigners, or as some are calling this group more recently, Student Leaders. We start with these kids because I believe they should be the key and focus of our ministry. They are the fruit of our labor and the future disciples with whom God has entrusted us. Our main job is to help them grow into the men and women of God that He desires for them to be, and it is our privilege to work with this strategic group.

Therefore, by definition, a Campaigner kid is a high school person who is committed to Christ and to reaching others in his or her school through the tool of our ministry. Campaigners is a meeting (usually held at least weekly) of a group of Campaigner kids for Bible study, fellowship, prayer, and strategizing for ministry. These committed kids will represent Christ and our ministry in their school and community. What happens or doesn't happen in their lives will be the way our ministry, and even perhaps the Christian faith, will be judged by the world around them. We cannot take this lightly. Many people may never give our faith a serious hearing because of the poor witness of those who claim to be the products of our ministry.

Kids are quick to judge. Based on their perception of those who claim to follow Christ, they will either judge Christianity as valid or not valid. We Christians can be like magnets. If we're the same as the world, we will be viewed as hypocrites and repel non-Christians because of our sameness. If, however, because of Christ in us, we are different from those in the world, non-Christians will be attracted to us in their search for God. Our difference cannot be surface differences. We cannot only define our uniqueness by what we don't do (i.e., we live the "cleaner" life) but rather by the way in which we proactively love those around us.

The difference of our lives should be in the way we love those around us, including the nonbelievers. Too often those of us in evangelical circles have sought to distinguish ourselves from the world by imposing varying forms of legalism on others and ourselves. This is not the message of the New Testament. We are to distinguish ourselves by our love for one another and those who don't know Christ. For this reason alone, we should make Campaigners our number one priority. This strategy would be true even if Jesus had not given us the model of discipleship; but He did give us this model, and He calls us to follow it.

At this point, however, it is advisable to make several specific observations about our Campaigner kids.

The first thing to realize about Campaigner kids is that, above all else, it is a privilege from the Lord to be entrusted with the spiritual growth of young Christians. This is somewhat comparable to the way it is a privilege to be entrusted with raising a child. I loved the privilege of nurturing our two sons as they grew to become God's men. The same may be said for our view of young believers. We wouldn't give birth to human babies and then desert them; and in the same way, we should not think about abandoning our spiritual children.

Second, many of the great rewards of the faith are in the blessings we receive from seeing our spiritual babes grow into maturity. It is great fun seeing these kids grow up in Christ and an awesome privilege to walk along side of them in the process. Perhaps because we don't know what to do with Campaigners or because we are more comfortable at contact work, or because we're not affirmed for our Campaigner work for whatever reason, most of us do not consider Campaigners our strong suit. But it should be. It needs to be the best thing we do—not the necessary evil we feel forced to do.

The following are a few suggestions.

BEGIN WITH THE RIGHT KIDS

First, it is imperative that you begin with the right kids. As Jim Collins points out in his excellent book, Good to Great, we should ask the question, "Do we have the right people on the bus?" Our experience is that it is best to start with one or two kids who are really committed to Christ, to reaching their friends, and to you. Begin looking for a couple of kids who are really going to give everything to making your ministry have the biggest impact in their high school. How do we identify these kids? Often we miss the kids God would use mightily because we are looking for the wrong things. Outward gifts and abilities are fine, but 1 Samuel 16:7 tells us how God picked King David: "for the Lord sees not as man sees; man looks on the outward appearance, but the Lord looks on the heart." We need to pick kids who first and foremost have a heart for Christ, as well as for sharing their love for Him with the world.

But we need to be careful here also. Remember that the verse says that it is God who looks on the inside. Too often we think that since God looks on the inside we should also, but that assumes that we have the same capabilities as God. It can be a dangerous thing for us to try to look on the inside of someone else (Dr. Kooistra was fond of saying, "the heart has no dipstick," but we can see the outward signs of a person who is passionate for Christ. Our role here is to be guided by His spirit in the same way in which He guided Samuel and listen to His voice as we are drawn to His kids.

FOLLOWERS

Second, it is helpful for these key kids to have some kind of "chemistry" with you so that they will follow you. If they are unwilling to follow you as the leader, then perhaps God has another leader they can follow. This is not to say that there has to be immediate, initial "cloning." That would present other problems; but they must be interested in following you on some level, or you will find yourself very frustrated with trying to lead someone who refuses to be led.

AVAILABILITY

Third, we should be looking for kids who are available to be used by God. Most kids with lots of gifts are already committed to other things, and our ministry will be just another activity competing for their time. Sometimes availability is more important than ability. My mentor, Jerry Johnson, used to say that if thirteen girls went out for the cheerleading squad and twelve made the cut, he wanted the one who didn't make the squad, because she was available and looking for something else to get involved in and give her life to. She had time.

When I first moved to Bethlehem, the Club I inherited was not having a meeting for Campaigners. After summer camp, they had tried to run a Campaigner meeting; but as I was told, kids had lost interest and they had abandoned the idea. I asked the leaders to go to each of the kids who they thought might still be interested in a time of growing in their walk with Christ and invite them to a meeting on a certain night. About fifteen kids showed up for that first Campaigner meeting. I laid out for them the vision we had for investing in those who wanted to grow in Christ and for impacting the school with Club. The next week, only five kids showed up. I asked God to raise up from that group just one guy to model the new things I was going to talk about each week. Doug was that kid.

Each week we met with those faithful five kids and talked about what it meant to really be a follower of Christ. The truth of giving ourselves away for the sake of others is so predominant throughout the Scripture that I had no trouble doing Bible study after Bible study on the subject. Week after week, I would teach from the Bible on servant leadership and having a heart for your friends. After a couple of weeks, Doug called me and began explaining parts of his new vision of reaching his friends that I had not communicated in Campaigners. I knew that he could only have reached this understanding because the Holy Spirit had given it to him and therefore, he was to be the kid that God wanted me to focus on. He and I did not initially "click," but after spending more and more time together, we built a solid friendship. He wound up only bringing a few kids to Club, but he was the model for an entire generation of future Campaigners kids. A year later, a new Christian told me the impact it made upon him when Doug—a pretty popular junior—said "Hi" to him, a sophomore, in the hall after having met him at Young Life. That kid thought, "What is different about these people that they even speak to me?" More importantly, he was God's choice, no matter how many kids he actually brought to Club. Doug was part of my sixtieth birthday party and that night man after man went up to Doug to thank him for the role he played in their coming to Christ. Literally hundreds of people know Christ because of Doug's role in that club.

Drew was another kid that no one would have picked. I know I certainly wouldn't have picked him. As a freshman he was scrawny, wore thick glasses, was slightly overbearing, and not particularly athletic. But God had great plans for Drew, and He used him in a tremendous way. Drew went with us to camp after his freshman year; and when he returned as a sophomore, he almost single-handedly built the Club we were just starting in his high school. Each week he reviewed his prayer list of about fifty kids and called each one to come to Young Life. We had Club in a home at the bottom of the hill where his neighborhood was located. Each week he would walk to the top of the hill with one other guy, and they would work their way down the hill stopping by each person's house to bring them to Club. He would walk in with twenty to thirty kids each week. With only forty kids in the Club, if he didn't bring his friends, we didn't have a Club. Drew had a heart for Christ and was willing to be used by Him.

Thirty of Drew's friends went to camp that next summer and twenty-six of them gave their lives to Christ. Greatly in part because of Drew's model, those twenty-six kids built a Club of 120 kids and became the base for the growth of an entire area. Additionally, most of those twenty-six kids are continuing to walk with Christ today and are significant leaders in His kingdom. Six years later, after three sets of leadership changes, the Club never missed a beat. The foundation was solid, and the modeling continued. In fact, the third generation of new Christians even trained the new leader after Debbie and I moved to St. Louis. But it didn't start with Drew, it started with Doug. Doug was the model that gave Drew the picture of what it meant to be a Campaigner who follows Christ and expends his life for others.

We would have never picked Drew or Doug, but God had great plans for them. God saw on the inside people willing to be used by Him. I believe God has lots of Drews and Dougs out there who we are missing because we are not looking for the right things in our "key" kids.

FOCUS ON A FEW

At this point, you may be asking yourself where to start. My advice is to look for a few kids who have a spiritual hunger and a spiritually motivated desire to reach their school—kids who you can see God shaping and molding, and who are ready to be used by Him. Walk with these kids the way Jesus walked with His disciples. Share your life experiences with them, and let them share their lives with you.

Consider the model of Jesus. Jesus did not meet with His disciples once a week to go through a lesson in the latest study guide; he lived his life with his disciples.

It's not my intention to demean devotional guides. I've written two of them myself and they can be great tools. But simply sitting with someone and working through a devotional book is not discipleship. Discipleship involves the investment of one life into another life, and that doesn't happen in a one-hour-a-week meeting. This may seem scary at first, and it involves vulnerability and risk, but our confidence is in Christ and we can proceed in faith.

Once you have identified the kids you are going to disciple, share your spiritual life with them. Share the great discoveries and answers to prayer as well as the hurts, doubts, and fears. Do not be detached and isolated; be real and vulnerable. Allow these kids to see your heart for the other kids in the school, and share your vision for reaching the school. As these kids begin to grow and reach out to their friends, the others in Campaigners will notice the model and begin to catch on. It's true that by concentrating on the spiritual pacesetters, you may lose some of the other kids at first because the pace is too much for them. The alternative however, is to set the pace to the lowest common denominator and lose the kids whose spiritual hunger is being starved by the rations of spiritual food you are providing for the spiritually anorexic.

My experience over and over has been that lukewarm kids who go away eventually return because of the same needs that brought them to Christ in the first place. It is helpful to remember the principle that one kid totally committed is better than twenty kids who are only half committed. You can depend on the one kid, and he is a good model. The twenty half-committed kids cannot be counted on and are rotten models who will reproduce, if they reproduce at all, other half- (or less) committed kids. Remember that "hot" kids will get other kids "hotter."

It is also helpful to set some kind of goals for your discipleship kids. You can start by taking a spiritual inventory of where they are and where you believe God wants you to take them in the next few years. What things about a deeper personal walk with Christ do they need to learn? What areas of leadership are they already familiar with, and what will be areas of growth for them? How will you help them allow Christ to permeate every aspect of their lives? These are some of the questions I ask about my discipleship kids. Then I think and pray for ways in which they will learn these invaluable life lessons while they are with us during their high school years. The greatest thing about a ministry that is Student Leader centered is that your Campaigners will learn great spiritual lessons from the experience of expending themselves for Christ and others through the vehicle of the Club. These spiritual lessons will last a lifetime.

THE MODEL OF JESUS

The idea of focusing on a few is a difficult concept to grasp, but remember that it was the strategy of Jesus and He was the model. Jesus loved and had compassion for the crowds. He wouldn't let the disciples send them away because He had compassion for them; and we see Jesus with the multitudes, feeding them, (twice) healing them, and loving them. This is the high school you work in.

He also had the large group of followers. This group would have included Mary, Martha, and Lazarus, among many others. Some were believers and some were not. Some were just curious and were just in the crowd because it was the place to be. This is your Club. There are lots of kids in your Club who are there because it is the fun place to be or because they are curious. It's great to have these kids come to Club and there will be Mary's, Martha's, and Lazarus's in your Club too. They are not insignificant to the ministry in your school, but they are also not part of the core group.

Jesus had a smaller group of twelve that he was really pouring his life into. They were living their lives with Him. They went where he went, experienced the miracles with Him, and listened to all of his teachings. They were His disciples, and they had a special place in His life and ministry. These are your Campaigners.

From that group, Jesus had the three: Peter, James, and John. He took them to the Mount of Transfiguration and left the others down below. They saw things the others did not, and they experienced things the others did not. They were separate from the others and everyone knew it. They were chosen in a different way from the others, and Jesus made a point of singling them out from the rest of the twelve and gave them deeper attention.

Finally, he had an even deeper relationship with the Apostle John—the disciple whom Jesus loved. He loved them all of course, but it is noteworthy that John was designated as "the disciple whom Jesus loved." It was a different relationship. They were closer. In Jesus's complete humanness, he needed a "best friend." He needed someone who would be different than the others. John would bear a different burden than the others; but with that burden came the deeper relationship with Jesus. It is important to note that Peter took the Gospel to the Jews and Paul (who wasn't part of the twelve and was converted after Jesus's resurrection) took the Gospel to the Gentiles. John took his relationship with Jesus to us all. When you read the Gospel of John, you see how completely different it is from the other three Gospel narratives. It is the remembering's of a best friend. It is John telling us the inner thoughts of his friend and the emotions of our Lord. Notice the number of times in the Gospel of John that he tells us what Jesus is thinking or feeling. He knew Jesus at a deeper level than the other disciples and shared that depth with the world.

We may be afraid that other Campaigners may become jealous and resentful if we focus on one or three, but we must trust the model of Jesus and allow God to deal with those who feel left out. Remember, Peter had this issue and asked Jesus what would happen to John. But Jesus told him, "It's not your problem." OK, that's my translation, but it is the essence of what Jesus said to Peter. Jesus wasn't insensitive to the other disciples; He was just letting them know that John had a different place in his life. This is not a call to insensitivity to the other Campaigners. We must encourage and embrace them as much as our time allows, but we cannot be spread evenly among them all.

I am looking for a few guys who will be pacesetters for the rest of the group. Kids who will be highly committed and give sacrificially of their time to the ministry and who are growing in the faith in a way that is a model to the rest. Most of the time, if we set the pace fast enough, there will only be a few who are willing to be committed at that level, and the reason for your selection of pacesetters will be obvious.

When we had fifty kids in Campaigners, there were three guys and three girls who were pacesetters and stood out from the rest of the pack. We privately called them the "All Stars," and we did special things with them. Deb and I (we were the only leaders) were highly committed to that group of All Stars. Once a month we did something special with them, such as going out to dinner or going away overnight together. It was a special relationship between the eight of us, and we were truly in it together.

One day they came to us and asked if we could pray together every day for the rest of their senior year (January to June). That's commitment! We agreed, and every day after school, at least some of them would come over to our house to pray for their friends, for the Club, the summer camp trip, and for the rest of the Campaigners. They even began to bring with them some of the new Christians who were underclassmen. In doing so, they were tremendous models and built a base of next generation Campaigners who would carry the Club long after the initial six had graduated.

This commitment to the ministry is most significant when you consider how frustrating most second semester seniors can be. It is no accident that this was the time when the Club grew the most.

THE CAMPAIGNER MEETING

When planning a Campaigner meeting, it's best to make it at a time when all or most can come, but it will cost them something. I love early morning before school Campaigner meetings. No one has a schedule conflict, and it costs them something near and dear—sleep! If school started at 8:00 a.m., we had Campaigners from 6:30–7:30am. We had breakfast together (something simple that they help pay for), and there is something great about seeing each other in the morning that brings us all together.

Second, I never make Campaigners issue oriented. I don't talk about drinking one week, dating the next and nuclear holocaust the next. Our goal is to teach kids the Scripture and how to discover its truths for themselves. Remember, our goal is to build men and women of God. The issues will change from year to year, but the Scripture remains the same. It is to the Scripture that they must come to get answers to life's questions long after they have left our ministry.

FOUR THEMES

My format has been to weave four themes through all that I teach in hope that these themes will be a foundation for greater spiritual growth after the kids leave high school. Those four themes are:

1) The view of a sovereign God and what it means to trust Him with our lives.

2) The importance of prayer, Bible Study, and fellowship.

3) The need to be involved in some type of ministry to others.

4) The significance of the question, "What are you going to give your life to?"

By spending time with Campaigner kids and determining what they need to hear in order to grow in their walk, I decide what specific scripture to look at. Most of the time, the Bible study for Campaigners comes from what I'm learning in my own devotional time with Christ. As I read and study the Scripture for myself, the ideas of how to relate what I'm reading to kids become a natural outgrowth. The list of issues may be different from one Campaigner group to another, but the key is to address the spiritual needs that are beneath the surface of every problem your kids may have. It is better for them to graduate established in a few spiritual truths than to have a little bit of knowledge about a lot of issues. Approximately one third of our meetings are spent studying the Scripture.[vii]

A second third of our time is spent talking about Club and sharing with each other. We talk about the response of their friends to Club, how our camp sell is going, how they are seeing God answer their prayers, and how we can help each other with the people we love. This all goes under the heading of "vision," and giving kids a vision for reaching their high school may be the most important aspect of a leader's job. We also share personal needs and requests, but that is limited, because deep sharing is usually not facilitated in large groups.

The last third of our time is spent praying for one another and for the people to whom we are giving ourselves. Sometimes this is done in small groups or we break into groups of males and females. Sometimes we break the groups by age. The point is that we become a praying group of people—for each other and for those we're sharing Christ with.

Prayer is one of the most important things we can teach our Christian kids. We have each kid pray out loud when he or she returns from camp so that together they can get over the fear of praying together. We teach them to make prayer lists and to learn the habit of a daily quiet time. Additionally, we have a day of prayer each semester for the whole area. The Lord has been teaching me not to have a demanding spirit, and we are trying to teach our kids to pour out their hearts to the Lord without demanding their will and ignoring His.

In some ways, our ministry is similar to a football team. God is the owner, He has hired me as head coach, and the Campaigner kids are the players. I love getting together with my team, enjoying one another, studying God's Word together, praying together, and charging up the team to work together toward the same goal. As you grow deeper in your relationships with these new brothers and sisters in the faith, you will probably look forward to meeting with your Campaigners the most.

CѰChapter FiveⱮꝊ

Contacts

Contact work has always been central to the mission of Young Life. Perhaps nothing we do better illustrates the principle of "going where kids are" and "winning the right to be heard" than contact work. The purpose of contacts is threefold. To begin with, contact work enables leaders to establish friendships with kids and become involved in their lives with the ultimate goal of proclaiming Christ to them and leading them to be disciples. We are not at the high school only to be a friend to kids. We are not a social welfare agency hoping to make bad kids good. (Remember, it is God who sanctifies each of us. It is not our job to be in the business of making anyone "good.") We are at the high school with the purpose of telling as many kids as we can about the love of God in Christ. In the process, we are also creating a model for Campaigners.

Contact work allows us to "see and be seen" at the high school. That is, in our role as head coach for our team of Campaigners, we have the opportunity to "scout" the field. We can help our Campaigners immeasurably by knowing the school where they will have ministry and pointing them in the right directions. We walk the campus, make our observations, see "who's who in the zoo," and bring an adult set of eyes to the everyday life of a high school. We watch kids and see how they interact with each other. We see who the leaders are, who follows whom, who is hurting, and who is lonely. We pray for the kids we see, and we ask the Lord to give us new eyes to see what is not easily apparent. We ask the Spirit to guide us and to give us insight so that we can have a coach's perspective on the school. Then we share that perspective with the team—with our Campaigners—and we talk about how best to reach the school.

We are also there to be seen by kids in the school so that as Campaigners bring them to Club, we will be familiar to them. This helps Campaigners in their role of following up the leader's talks, because the talks will not have come from a stranger. We do not do contacts so that leaders can reach an entire school by themselves through their relationships with kids; contacts are done primarily as a model and an aid to Campaigners.

When I stand in the kids' section of the football game and talk with kids, I want them to ask the Campaigner kid I'm with, "Who is that guy?" I want him to tell his friends, "That's Bob. He's the Young Life leader. You know I've been asking you to come to Young Life. That guy is the leader." If his friends don't say, "OK, he's pretty cool, I'll check it out," or something like that, then I have not helped my Campaigner. I should have stayed home.

One of my first jobs after moving to St. Louis as the Area Director was to assume the leadership of the only viable Club in the area at that time. Going to the high school for contacts, I walked around and checked out the various school activities. Wanting to build relationships with kids with whom I could work and disciple for three or four years, I decided to follow the junior varsity soccer team. As I watched the team, one of the kids (Brian) began to stick out in my mind. I believe that God was leading me to begin praying for Brian, but the fact that a group of about ten girls kept yelling his name didn't hurt.

An advantage of going to JV games is that very few other people attend, and you "stand out." Consequently, I continued seeing these girls yelling Brian's name, and I got to know them. Soon it became the natural thing to cheer for Brian and the other guys on the team that these girls knew. Soon I was saying, "Hi," to Brian, and we were talking about the games, how he played, etc.

In Campaigners I asked if anyone knew Brian. The Campaigner group that I inherited consisted mostly of juniors and seniors in "the popular crowd" who had been with the Club prior to my moving to St. Louis. Getting to know freshmen was not on their agenda! After mentioning Brian to them, I challenged them to see if any of them could figure out who Brian was and actually invite him to Club. They never did, but in the process they discovered how self-centered they were. (An aside: About six months later, one of the seniors in that group said, "I think that Brian kid is my brother's best friend.")

One guy did invite some other freshmen, and this was a start. One of the freshmen he invited to Club that spring was a guy named Jeff who went to camp that summer and gave his life to Christ. In God's providence, Jeff's best friend was a Christian guy on the soccer team named Bret who had never shared his faith with Jeff. When Bret saw that Jeff became a Christian, he wanted to know how he could get involved with Young Life so that more of his friends could come to Christ. Bret and I began to pray for the soccer team, and Brian's name was at the top of our list. All year, Bret asked Brian to come to Club, and each week Brian had an excuse and never came. However, many other guys from the team did come, and Brian began to wonder about Young Life and me and what we were all about. In the process, I got to know Brian better and better, and we became friends.

At the start of Brian's junior year, we were sitting in the stands together watching soccer, and Brian turned to me and said, "Where is Young Life this week?"

I said, "It's okay, Brian; you don't have to come to Young Life for us to be friends." He said that he really did want to come, and I told him to find out the details from Bret. At that point, it was key that I not be the one to give him all the details. To do so would have been to cut Bret out of the process, thereby preventing his seeing God use him in Brian's life.

It is important to point out here that I made it a rule to never invite a kid to Club myself. I did not want kids at school to think I was there just to recruit them to my thing, and I didn't want my Campaigner kids to think that I would do the inviting for them. I didn't want to put a kid in the awkward position of having to say no to me or to lie to me. I wanted there to be no strings attached to my being at school. I broke that rule once and I was sorry I did.

Brian came to Club and loved it. He came all fall, and even brought another friend from the soccer team with him. They both went on our winter trip to Florida. We had a great time at Disney World, and each night in our cabin time it was Brian who made sure we talked about the message he had heard that morning in Club. On the last day, we sat and talked about where he was with Christ. He told me that his family had never been to church (I already knew that.) and that he'd never before heard the message of Christ. It was too much too fast, and he was not ready for a decision. I told him that it was his decision and regardless of his choice, we would still be friends. Because I had to be in San Diego the next day, I was unable to ride the bus from Florida back to St. Louis. When I called home to see how the bus ride had gone, I was told that one of the Campaigners who had gone around Disney World with us all week had prayed with Brian on the bus, and Brian gave his life to Christ!

A few weeks later, Brian and I sat together at a fast food place, and he told me how he had struggled with giving his life to Christ. He shared the great help of his Campaigner friend as he choked out his prayer of commitment through the tears of his brokenness. It came as no surprise that when we resumed Club in January, Brian brought three of his friends. No one had to tell him to bring other people; he had seen the model and was only doing what had been done for him.

What an awesome God we serve who allows His people to be involved in the process of leading others to Him. I am glad that God put Brian on my heart, that He brought Campaigner kids along with me to share in the witness, and that He encouraged our faith by seeing the power of His Spirit in the conversion of souls. I am also grateful that we are encouraged to start this tremendous process with contact work.

The following year as Brian and Bret moved up to the varsity soccer team, I continued to hang out with the guys on the JV squad. I got to know the coach, and at the end of the season, he invited me to the banquet and honored me in front of the whole team and their parents. We took twelve guys from that team to our Disney World trip that year, and many of those guys responded to Christ. I thought back and realized it all began with God leading me to pray for Brian.

It is worth pointing out that I never went to school while classes were in session. My principle was that I would only go to school at times when anyone from the general public could be there. I didn't want a confrontation with an administrator about the legality of my being on campus. It was a battle I didn't want or need to fight. One spring I was watching freshmen baseball and the coach asked if any of the parents knew how to keep score. I told him I could, and he was thrilled to have me help him out. At every game, I sat in the dugout with the team and got to really know the guys on the team. It was an awesome time of contacts with those guys, and many of them came to Club and camp. I was able to do plenty of contact work by being at after school activities. But what if you just can't be at the school at all? What if circumstances prevent you from being present at the school? That only happened to me one year.

For a complex set of circumstances, I did not go to the high school for most of a year. We became very creative with finding ways for me to meet kids away from the high school. There were other community events, movie theaters, etc., and, fortunately, because we had a Campaigner-centered Club, the Club actually grew that year. The Campaigners knew that it was all up to them to make the Club happen—they weren't going to get any help from the leaders—and they rose to the occasion.

Chapter Six

CLUB

A great Club can be compared to the brackish water that flows around the point at Malibu. The Malibu Club is Young Life's magnificent property in British Columbia, Canada. The camp sits at the intersection of fresh water and salt water. Fresh water from the mountains flows down into the Jarvis Inlet that intersects with salt water from the Pacific Ocean. That point of intersection is known as "brackish" water.

A great Club should be like that water; a mix of Christian kids and their non-Christian friends, coming together to have a fun time and consider the significant things of God.

The purpose of Club is to serve Campaigners in their ministry to their friends as well as to provide a format for presenting the Gospel to large groups of kids.

That sentence more than any other sentence in this book has caused the greatest amount of discussion among staff. It may be the biggest hurdle we have to conquer, but it is key to really changing from a leader-centered ministry to a Campaigner-centered ministry. If we say we want to serve Campaigners but keep control of the Club meeting in the hands of the leaders, then we have sacrificed our philosophy on the altar of our program.

We need to view Club as a place to be used by Campaigners in order to better enable them to present the Gospel to their friends in a relational way. As stated previously, all of our forms should serve our functions. Our functions include Campaigners growing in Christ as well as masses being reached in a relational way. Our Clubs must support these purposes. Therefore, Club should be designed to meet the relational needs of kids as well as the spiritual needs of kids.

I should note here that this does not represent the typical approach in Young Life that I grew up with. Most of us have seen Club as a place where Campaigners are really not necessary and may even be getting in the way of what the leaders are trying to do. In the Club I was in as a kid, the Campaigners had very little to do with the Club.

In my view however, Club should be a tool for Campaigners to use—an extension of the relationships they are building with their friends in school. It cannot be a performance by the leaders each week designed to compete with television, movies, computer games or the Internet. The two great attractions of a Young Life Club should be the message of Jesus Christ and the relationships with the people who are there. Those two things together cannot be duplicated by the technology age.

As our culture becomes more and more impersonal, the message of Christ, in the context of the Young Life Club, will be one of the few places where the value of a person is affirmed.

This cannot be overstated. Kids are facing all kinds of stimulus today from many directions. Places where the truth of Christ—the truth that is Christ—is presented are too few. To present that truth in a caring, loving, relational manner is a unique privilege for us, and we should take hold of it strongly.

It seems like every year a kid came up to me after Club, shaking his head in bewilderment and saying, "I don't know why, but Young Life is always the highlight of my week." I know why. It's Christ in the lives of other people, and it cannot be duplicated by anything the world has to offer. One night a mother called to say that her son didn't seem to be interested in anything else in life, but on Thursday nights, he came alive for Young Life. It is Christ in the lives of Campaigners, sharing their light with those in darkness that makes Young Life Club the highlight of many kids' weeks and ultimately their entire lives.

Everything we do in Club (the music, humor, and message) should be designed so that Campaigners and leaders can use the evening as part of the relational process of sharing the Gospel. The real "action" in Club happens on the floor between kids and their friends. One night I had laryngitis and couldn't lead songs. I went to Club and sat on the floor with a kid I had known from contacts at school. We had an awesome time of fun and laughter together. It reminded me again that the real thrill is person to person, sitting on the floor, singing the songs together, laughing at Minutes together, praying for the people around me as the speaker presents the message, and just being with my friends.

Club should be more Campaigner-centered than leader-centered. Kids should go home remembering the great time they had interacting with their friends. The role of the leaders is to facilitate that interaction. It must not be a show put on each week by the leaders because to do so robs Campaigners of the ownership of the Club. When a Club is "leader-centered," then the people being served the most are the leaders not the Campaigners.

Our role as leaders is to serve Campaigner kids. The format must enable them to have ministry with their friends. (Note Appendix A, "The Twenty-Three Things Campaigners Do the Day of Club" as a tool to help Campaigners understand how to best use the tool of Club.)

WARNING: excellent Club mechanics must go hand in hand with Campaigner ownership of Club.

I'm afraid that many people have dismissed the traditional Young Life Club as being obsolete. They say that classic Club doesn't work with kids anymore. Typically, they have missed the key ingredient of a great Club: Campaigner ownership. By the same token, some have tried to use Campaigners to do the ministry without providing a great Club for them to bring their friends to. They too, have become discouraged, as kids have not done what was expected. I believe that when we ask kids to risk themselves by bringing their non-Christian friends to a Christian meeting, we better make sure it is the best Christian meeting we can provide—one they won't be ashamed of the next day in school. A

Campaigner kid should walk into lunch the next day and have his or her friends say, "Thanks for taking me to Young Life last night. That was awesome!"

CLUB MECHANICS

Great mechanics—or the lack of them—can make or break a Young Life Club. They are important because excellent mechanics are a key way in which we serve Campaigner kids who are risking themselves with their friends. The following are some suggestions in making Club the high point of the week for each kid who attends.

MUSIC–Music in a Young Life Club has several purposes. It is primarily an emotional tool. Music is fun, it elicits emotion, and it is a window to the soul. An important question to ask after singing in Club is, "How did the kids feel about the singing?" The music should bring people together. Kids should sing songs that are fun to sing and that make those who might ordinarily feel "outside" the group feel as if they belong. I am constantly amazed when I hear leaders saying that kids don't like to sing anymore. Kids are singing all the time! They're singing to the latest music on the radio, and they are more aware of music as an art form than they ever were thirty years ago. I believe that kids love to sing but that we're not singing the right songs.

Finding the right songs takes a lot of work. You've got to find music that is singable in a group, that has appropriate words, and that is just fun to sing. For every thirty songs you consider, you might find one song that will work in Club. It takes a lot of work, but it is worth it. I had a core set of songs that I knew worked. Those ten to fifteen songs were sung in every Club I ever led. In addition to those songs, every year I searched for new songs. I was listening to hundreds of songs—many recommended by Campaigner kids—to determine if a song would be great for Club. Every week we sang from the same list of about twenty-five songs. I never felt the need to do a completely new set of songs every week, and I think kids enjoyed knowing that they were going to be singing familiar songs at Club each week.

I am a baby boomer, and it is my contention that because of demographics, the music of the baby boomers will be with us for a long time. The music from the '60s is constantly being revived by current artists and is heard in current movies and television. Some of the best music I've heard in Club is music from that era. You might want to begin your music search by looking at what songs from the '60s and '70s are being popularized in contemporary culture.

The first set of songs should be up-tempo, have a beat that practically demands clapping, and be easily recognizable to most of the kids. A great song is one the toughest kids in the room will find irresistible to their participation. I loved it when my Campaigner guys from the football team would bring their friends to Club. Those tough guys would stand in the back—too cool to be part of it. Then the music started, and after a couple of songs, they were singing. Loudly. That is great music and it breaks down the barriers, brings them into the group, and serves the Campaigner who brought them. Here's a hint: great songs make you clap on two and four—the rhythm of a great song is felt on the off beats. Try to find songs that have the kind of rhythm that requires them to be sung with clapping on the offbeat.

As kids sing, the emotional walls begin to crumble, and they feel more comfortable with being there. When kids sing they move from being observers to participants. They then begin to feel that they are accepted and are part of the Club. The first set of songs should reach a feverish, rowdy, emotional pitch just before Minutes. I was once at a camp where the singing was so good that I thought the kids were not going to let us stop singing. These were tough kids who were having a great time and were letting go of a lot of emotion during the singing and they didn't want it to stop.

The first song after Minutes should be a "transition" song that is not too slow and not too fast. It transitions to slow songs and moves the emotion of the night to the next thing. After the transition song, the next few songs should set up the talk. They should be slower in tempo and result in settling the crowd. This does not mean, however, they should lack in emotional intensity. Most of us have had the experience of being moved deeply by an emotionally powerful slow song. These kinds of songs strike an even deeper emotion that is powerful in setting up the talk. The emphasis in this second set should be on a more peaceful, reflective mood when compared with the rowdy mood of the first set. The message of these songs should "introduce" the talk that will follow by carrying the message of Christ that will soon be proclaimed verbally by the speaker. The words in these songs should introduce the concepts of God, Christ, man's need and redemption. This is not to say that these songs should be too religious or "praise songs," but they should begin to introduce the concepts the speaker will be talking about. Often kids will remember these songs, and their message, when they might forget the talk.

MINUTES–When Jim Rayburn was designing his first "Club," he decided to include a parody of the traditional reading of the Club minutes. This parody, actually one of his crazy skits, was what we now call "Minutes," or "participation skit."

This is a time for kids to laugh and have fun doing things they would not ordinarily do. This is not a time for leaders to entertain kids. Kids should be in front of the group and involved in the fun.

As leaders, we must be creative and develop Minutes that do not humiliate kids, but at the same time do have them shedding a little of their "coolness" in order to have some fun. Both the choice of Minutes and the selection of the kids who will be in them require careful thought and advance preparation. My favorite Minutes are the ones that more closely resemble "party games," where kids are brought up front to participate in a race or relay of some sort (usually messy). In some areas these are called "participation skits." The action is fast and furious, and it captures the attention of the whole room.

The measuring stick for a great Minutes is if kids are still talking about it the next day in school and for weeks to come. I want kids who were not at Club to think they missed something great by not seeing the Minutes. One year I got a call from a parent who was very upset and wanted to see me. This very nice Christian woman came over and put a copy of the school newspaper in front of me. On the cover was a story about Young Life and a picture of a couple of kids in Minutes. She looked at me with disgust and said, "What does this have to do with the Christian faith?" My first thought was, "That was a great Minutes!" It had nothing to do with the Christian faith, and everything to do with a great Club.

TALK–The purpose of the talk is to present the Gospel of Christ clearly, in a manner that adolescents will understand, and to which they may respond. This verbal communication of the Gospel should be short (no longer than twenty minutes),

81

clear (no ambiguous philosophy), faithful to the Word of God (man's wisdom cannot replace God's Word), should not contain any "religious" words, and, of course, it should relate to kids. They should see its relevance to their world and to their need. Examples and stories to illustrate points are useful, but if done incorrectly, they will hinder the message. We have a rare opportunity to talk to kids for a few moments about the most significant things of life. We must be careful in our preparation to consider what will reach and stay with kids after they've left Club.

Your talks should follow a progression. When I came into Young Life, the standard progression was: Person of Christ, Man's Need, Work of Christ, Response. I used that progression for the first semester and added my own for the second semester. That progression asked four questions:

1) Who is Jesus Christ?

2) What did He do?

3) Why did He do it?

4) What does it mean to us today?

As we have become a more secular society, you may have to start back with questions about the existence of God and develop your own progression. The point is that you develop a progression of talks that serve your Campaigners. The progression should enable Campaigners to have significant conversations with their friends. On the drive home, or the next day at school, or after practice, or at lunch, your Campaigner kids should be able to say to the friends they brought, "What did you think of what the leader had to say last night?" and have a significant conversation with their friends.

Difficult though it is, the speaker must speak to the kid who has come for the first time as well as the one who has been there every week for a semester. Kids should want to hear more and return next week. In order to serve Campaigners, the talk should contain information that can be used by Campaigners as they converse with their non-Christian friends. Our goal is that the talk will be a starting point for further discussion by Campaigners and their friends as they sit at McDonalds after Club, drive home, talk at school the next day or stand around at a party on the weekend. The talk is a catalyst for further discussion and should be designed as such.

I liked to begin my talks with a summary of what happened at school in the past week in a kind of late night talk show monologue. If there was something to joke about, I made the joke. If there was something to celebrate, we celebrated. It was a way of letting kids know that this is part of their high school experience, and I knew what was going on at their school.

From the monologue I moved to a story or an illustration of what I was going to be talking about that night. I told the story as quickly and succinctly as I could yet gave plenty of color and detail to make it interesting. People remember stories and pictures more than they remember outlines. Try to paint a picture for them of the story you are telling.

After the introduction/story/illustration, I would relate it to something in the life of Jesus. I might say, "In the life of Jesus, there was an event that relates to the story I just told you." Then I would open the Bible and read the event to them. I would select only the key part they needed to hear. I didn't want them to get bored with a long passage of Scripture, I just wanted them to know that it was from the Bible.

Lastly, I gave them a conclusion. Something to think about and maybe even a question to ponder. I tried to bring it back to the story I told in the beginning and relate it to their lives. I wanted them to think about their lives, their eternity, their condition before God and why any of that mattered to them.

I finish by thanking them for coming and letting them know where we'll be next week. That's it. Twenty minutes tops. If there is follow-up to be done, then it is for the Campaigners to do. My job is to set the table. Campaigners can serve the meal.

One day early in my career I had a Campaigner kid come up to me after my talk and said, "Don't ever give that talk again. That was awful." This was a kid who had been involved from the start of the Club and he knew what he was talking about. I had not served him well. He was right. I thought about that talk a lot and where I had gone wrong. I apologized to him and worked hard to never disappoint a Campaigner kid again.

CONTEXTUALIZATION

When I moved to Canada, I had no idea what to expect in terms of relating the Gospel to kids who had grown up in a totally post-Christian culture. In the United States—even in the Northeast—there was still a context of Christianity. Kids still had a reference point for church and had heard some of the "Jesus stories." But in Canada—as in Europe—those reference points had been lost. On our first outreach camp, we presented the Gospel in the same sequence we always had in the States. It was like speaking to Martians. Kids heard the words but didn't understand a thing we were saying and none responded to the Gospel. They were nice, and didn't hate us, but they didn't respond. It was as if they had heard an interesting set of lectures.

During the post-camp analysis, we concluded that the biggest problem with the post-Christian culture is that it is based on relativism, and there is no absolute truth. As leaders were engaging kids every week in Club, they were discovering that the biggest hurdle to get over was that these kids did not have a baseline of truth in their lives from which they could hear the Gospel. So the second year we presented the Gospel in the context of "truth." We asked questions like, "Is there such a thing as truth?" "What kinds of truth are there?" "What is true about us?" and "What is true about God?" Instead of blank stares, we got anger. These kids were now angry at us for challenging at a very deep level all that they had ever known. None responded to Christ.

At the post-camp evaluation, we went back to the drawing board. We asked the question, "What is most important to these kids?" The answer: friends. For high school kids, what their peer group and friends think, is everything. One of the reasons a relational ministry works so well with high school kids is because it is a time in their lives when they are really forming their first deep relationships and they are discovering how to navigate the relationship waters. We decided to build the talk sequence around the concept of relationships. The relationship with one's self, the relationship with others, the broken relationships (sin), the relationship with God, and the relationship with Jesus, who is the one who can bridge the relationship gap between man and God. Kids ate it up. They finally heard the Good News in a way that they could relate to, and it made sense to them. Many kids responded to Christ on that trip, and it was the beginning of growing the ministry in Ontario.

It is incumbent upon us to contextualize the Gospel, and to do that, we have to know the culture we are working with and think about how to bring the truth of God's salvation to the audience we are attempting to reach. Every week your Club talk should engage the culture with the Gospel in a way that makes sense to them and that they can relate to.

SKITS

You might notice that I have said nothing about skits in my night of Club. That is because I never did them. I didn't do them for three reasons. First, I'm not good at them. There was no reason for me to spend the time and energy on something that was not essential to the Club and that I was never going to be good at. Second, I think most are really not that funny. Kids are exposed to very sophisticated humor today, and most of the skits I've seen are pretty lame at best. Lastly, no matter how good you are, they take a tremendous amount of time and creative energy to do, and that is time and energy you don't have. It would be far better for you to devote that time and energy to your Campaigners, contacts, your talk, or some personal down time. I always hated to see leaders stressed out before Club because they were still working on the skit, and they were dreading having to come up with another new one for the next week.

Keep your Club as simple as you can. Have a set number of songs, a great set of Minutes, and creatively relate to kids with your talk. A simple Club will enable you to enjoy it more and cause your Campaigners to have more fun.

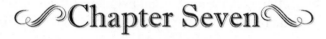

Chapter Seven

Camp

The next form to be discussed is camp. Young Life has fantastic properties and the commitment to excellence sets the standard. The challenge becomes how to use these camps in a manner consistent with the rest of our ministry philosophy so that camps serve the mass, relational, and disciplevangelism principles. The camping experience should be a complement to, not a contradiction of, our daily ministry. Camp should be another tool for Campaigners and leaders to use in the proclamation and discipleship of others. Camp cannot be viewed as simply a factory for mass conversions. It must be seen as a vehicle for providing Campaigners and leaders with isolated time away from everyday life to be with the people with whom they are already relationally connected.

The shared experience at camp between a Campaigner and his or her friend is a great part of the foundation for the proclamation of the Gospel by that Campaigner. The ultimate goal for a camp trip is to have the Gospel communicated verbally and non-verbally by our Campaigner kids to their friends. The message of Christ is to be passed on from one life to another as Paul says in 2 Timothy 2:2, "And what you have heard from me before many witnesses entrust to faithful men who will be able to teach others also." When the camp is designed to help Campaigners lead their friends to Christ, the camp experience better facilitates the presentation of the Gospel. The net result of this kind of experience will be seen generation after generation as Campaigners model what was modeled to them and continue to lead their friends to Christ.

We have traditionally believed that the model for camping was a leader who took non-Christian kids to camp. There is always a debate regarding whether or not Christian kids have a place at camp. If, however, we only rely on leaders to bring kids to camp and the camp team to lead them to Christ, we have limited ourselves to the number of people to whom the leaders can minister. If we see our job as enabling Campaigners to lead their friends to Christ, then the number of kids we can reach is only limited to the day of Christ's return.

One obvious problem created here is the dilemma of Christian kids returning to camp multiple times. I am an advocate of bringing "repeaters," if they are the right Campaigners who have a clear understanding of what their role at camp is and have been trained to lead their friends to Christ.

The program at camp it should be structured to encourage building relationships between Campaigners and their friends, as well as between leaders and kids. Camp should not be so highly programmed that Campaigners see their role as thwarted by the program. In order for Campaigners to have opportunities to share Christ with the friends they bring, we need to think about everything we do—the way we run the program, the kinds of properties we purchase, the kinds of tables we put in the dining room, everything—from the perspective of "Does this help Campaigner kids share Christ with their friends?" We must look at the entire week and make sure that what we do encourages the principles of relational evangelism.

The camp week should be limited in the amount of time spent in programed activities and be built around more free time. The week needs to involve activities available for Campaigner kids to hang out with their friends doing the things their friends are interested in doing. In this context, the campers can choose the activities, their involvement, and with whom they will be involved. This also offers the most desirable environment for the one-on-one sharing essential to the proclamation of the Gospel. One of my favorite things over the years was the Sunfish sailboats at camp because a Campaigner kid could take his friend out sailing and the shared experience caused the relationship to grow.

The proclamation should be a shared experience between what happens up front—the speaker, the role-play, the leaders—and the Campaigner kids. If the proclamation comes only from the camp staff, it will only impact one generation. If Campaigners share this responsibility, the impact is multigenerational because of the modeling that takes place.

Many people have told us that Christian kids are too immature to share their faith in Christ. This does not mesh with our experience. The message from an immature kid may not be precise and polished (which is the reason we have speakers and leaders), but there is no substitute for the genuineness of the relationship that an individual kid has with the friends he has brought to camp. The reality of what Christ has done in each of our lives is the most powerful testimony we can give. Over my twenty-two years in the ministry, I have seen many kids lead their friends to Christ. I believe that God uses these kids as much as He uses any leader. We must learn to trust God to use kids as His servants and allow them to experience Christ in their lives for themselves.

When we designed out Disney World trip, we did so because we felt a need to do a major winter camp that was just as good as the summer camp experience. I had gotten to know a group of guys on the baseball team, and they were never going to go to summer camp. They were not going to give up their dream of playing college baseball for a week at camp no matter how great the camp was. It just didn't seem right to me that we were telling them that the only opportunity to go to a great camp was not available to them unless they gave up their baseball careers. So we thought about the other options and what we could do in the break between Christmas and New Year's. We thought about a ski trip but rejected it for two reasons. First, not every kid can ski or wants to learn. It didn't make sense to limit our outreach to only kids who could ski. Second, we felt that the core activity of skiing did not facilitate great relational time between Campaigners and the friends they would bring.

For example if a guy brings a friend who is a much better skier than he is, then he won't see his friend all day. We wanted to honor the principle of Campaigners leading their friends to Christ, so we rejected the ski trip for that reason.

Disney World worked for us because:

1) Any kid can walk around Disney—or be wheeled around in a wheel chair, as we've done many times—and have a great time.

2) The Campaigner kids can spend the entire day with their friends.

3) We would not have to create an entire week of programming—program–Disney has done that for us.

We decided to wipe the slate clean and build the camp experience from the ground up on the principle that Campaigner kids would lead their friends to Christ. We had Club in the morning because we wanted to stay in the parks until they closed. We got back to camp from the park too late for cabin times, so most of the time we didn't have them. We would trust our Campaigner kids to talk to their friends and not need a cabin time. We had a "twenty minutes" and an invitation to respond to Christ, but we did not have a "say-so."

When I first got involved in Young Life, I loved the "say-so," but after several years, I began to question the whole thing. I don't really have violent objections to it, but I do have some questions. I spent too many bus rides with a group of kids who did not stand up and then huddled in the back of the bus just surviving the twenty-four-hour ride back to St. Louis, knowing they didn't do what we wanted them to do. It was painful. I also saw kids stand up and then show no sign whatsoever of Christ in their lives. So I began to ask why we did this.

I think it is good for a new believer to proclaim his faith publicly, but I also want that public affirmation to be away from the emotional high of camp. So we did our "say-so" when we got back home. A week after camp, we had our first All-Area Campaigners, and that's when we did our "say-so." The Campaigner kid who led his friend to Christ brought his friend to the "say-so." It was a week after camp, and if the commitment was real it was sticking by then.

I'm not saying that this is the only way to do it or that the "say-so" at camp is not valid. I am simply asking some questions and encouraging some creative thinking around all of the things we take for granted.

Those Disney camps were fantastic. There are many stories of kids sharing their faith with their friends while standing in line at "Space Mountain," "Tower of Terror," or some other ride. There are great stories of kids having dinner with their friends in a restaurant in Disney and talking about the talk that morning and sharing their faith—a different kind of cabin time.

Near the end of the week, we spent an entire day in camp and that is when most of the really significant conversations happened, and kids were responding to the Gospel. The last night of the trip was New Year's Eve. In the midst of the fireworks and celebration, our kids were celebrating not only a new year, but a new life in Christ, and our Campaigner kids were celebrating with their friends.

On one of those trips, I did not have the privilege of leading any of the non-Christian kids to Christ. My Campaigner guys brought their friends, shared with each of them, and those kids gave their lives to Christ without my involvement. This was a first for me, and I didn't enjoy it very much. What I did like was the fact that I could see the fruit of my ministry being reproduced in the lives of others. Kids whom I had led to Christ were leading others to Christ. Their own relationship with the Lord grew as a result of seeing Him be faithful in their lives. It is no wonder that so many of those kids continued on in their faith in college and are still having a great impact for Christ today.

One of the guys from that Florida trip called from the Naval Academy a couple of years later to tell me that after leading two of the guys in his company to Christ, they now had ten guys in the Bible study he'd started, and they were going to start another. It was a model he had learned as a freshman in high school, when a senior shared Christ with him.

Chapter Eight

Alumni

After walking with kids for several years while they were in high school, it did not seem right to simply drop them when they graduated and went on to college or university. As I looked at the Scripture, I realized that the principle implored there was one of continuing to walk with people. I realized that if I was committed to the principle of people being more important than program, then I had to continue to care about the people who came through our ministry, even though they may be leaving the existing situation.

Looking back at my own miserable spiritual existence during college, I thought a lot about what would have helped me during those years. I thought a great deal about the reasons I had drifted away from the faith and what would have helped me to grow in my relationship with Christ. As a result, we began an Alumni program.

The first step was to put together a college prep course for our senior Campaigners. The goal was to help our Campaigner kids be aware of the battles they were going to face when they went off to college and to give them some spiritual foundations from which to address those battles. I gathered together some of my friends who were on the Young Life staff, and we went away for five days to put together an outline that would address these issues. We asked the question, "What are the ten most important issues we want our senior Campaigners to deal with before they go off to college?" From that time together, we developed the "Principles of Kingdom Life" course that we used with our senior Campaigners.

The course brought together senior Campaigners from all the Clubs in the area for ten weeks in the spring semester and gave us a chance to really challenge our seniors in their walk with Christ as they prepared for college. The course also gave them a sense of belonging to the area, as well as a broader vision of what we are about. We asked them to stop participating in their regular Campaigner group for two reasons. First, we didn't want their "senioritis" to affect the underclassmen in Campaigners and second, those underclassmen now looked around the room, realized they were the new leaders, and began to take on the mantle of leadership.

From this course grew several other forms. We developed an Alumni Club and Bible Study groups during summer months when college kids were home from school. For many kids, the summer and semester breaks are the only times they have to "recharge" their spiritual batteries, so we wanted to make sure we provided an opportunity for them to do that. Many kids go to schools that don't have great

Christian fellowship groups or, for various reasons, they don't get involved in one. For these kids, college is a very difficult time spiritually, and I wanted to have a place they could come back to and be in fellowship for at least the time they were home. I wanted to remind them that they were Christians and that there were other people who believed the same things that they believed, even if it felt like they were the only ones at college.

During the academic year, all Alumni received a weekly newsletter[viii] with news of the area on one side of the page and a devotional on the other. This enabled the kid who was struggling in college to have contact with something spiritual at least once a week. Today of course there are all kinds of electronic and social media ways of staying in touch with your alumni, and I encourage you to take advantage of them. The important thing is that you make the effort to continue to be connected to your alumni.

At Thanksgiving we had a special Alumni Reunion Club, and at Christmas break we did an Alumni Retreat. Additionally, we staffed the work crew for our Disney World trip with our college alumni.

During my last summer in St. Louis, I decided to pull out all the stops with alumni. We had a weekly large group meeting that began with volleyball at 6:00 p.m., then Club at 7:30 p.m., and everyone hanging out or going to get ice cream afterward. Each week we had either a leader in the area or a professor from Covenant Seminary speak. Let me tell you, those were great Clubs!"

Additionally, during the week there were small-group Bible studies led by the alumni themselves. We worked through a book, and on Sunday night, I met with the various leaders of the small groups and we discussed the chapter of the book they would be talking about in their small group that week.

Every couple of weeks they did a social event, and at the end of the summer, they did a weekend retreat. It was almost entirely led by alumni, and it was my favorite summer in the ministry.

Each year I also tried to spend a couple of weekends on a college campus. I wanted to go see our kids and live in their world for a day or two. It reminded me of the environment our Campaigner kids would soon be facing.

The alumni part of our ministry became a tremendous blessing. We were able to continue the relationships built during high school, and we benefited from the encouragement of seeing so many of our kids involved, often in leadership positions with other Christian groups. These kids were investments who also became future Young Life leaders, committee, and donors.

When we fail to commit a little extra effort toward maintaining alumni contact, we have let go of one of our greatest resources. The benefits will well outweigh the costs. One key to organizing all of this is that the responsibilities must be delegated. Obviously one person cannot do it all. With minimal guidance from the staff, alumni themselves ran the summer program. We found that if we spent our time investing in kids in high school, we would have plenty of quality people to choose from to help run the Alumni Program.

Chapter Nine

Conclusion

In closing, I must acknowledge that much of my philosophy of ministry is a result of reading and studying The Lost Art of Disciple Making by LeRoy Eims of the Navigators, and Disciple by Juan Carlos Ortiz. These two books convinced me of the Biblical mandate to focus on disciples. The question for me was how to combine that focus with traditional Young Life, the ministry I had known all through high school and felt called to as a leader. The answer came in giving shared spiritual partnership to Christian kids.

One of the most key sections of Scripture for me has been Mark 8:34–38. Jesus says,

"If any man would come after Me let him deny himself and take up his cross and follow me. For whoever would save his life will lose it and whoever loses his life for My sake and the Gospel will save it. For what does it profit a man to gain the whole world and forfeit his life? For what can a man give in return for his life? For whoever is ashamed of Me and My words in this adulterous and sinful generation of him will the Son of Man also be ashamed when He comes in the glory of the Father with the holy angels."

The idea that we take up our cross to follow Jesus is congruent with the idea that we must lay down our lives to follow Jesus. Jesus does not ask us for part of our life, He asks us for our entire life. When Jesus talks with the rich young ruler, He tells him to give up everything he has and to follow Him. To proclaim the Gospel of Christ to kids (or anyone) is to ask them to give their lives to Christ. That is, to give their entire lives to Christ.

Our job as leaders in God's community is to help other people experience Christ. My job was to equip and train volunteers to have ministry so that they would experience Christ. The job of a Club leader is to equip and train Campaigner kids to have ministry so that they experience Christ. The job of the leader is to give ministry away, while modeling it himself.

As I have presented the thoughts in this book to many Young Life staff, a consistent reaction has been that, while the ideas make sense and seem to be grounded Biblically, they are afraid to try this approach for fear that it will not produce the results they want from their Clubs.

We must trust Biblical principles to guide our means for ministry, even if they do not produce the results we desire right away. I began as a leader with the conviction to trust God with the numbers, and I was committed to following His way of investing my life in kids. What I believe He has shown me is that by obeying Him, the numbers will come. Numbers are never the issue; trusting God is always the issue. God is faithful and cares more about kids then I do. I must trust that as long as I am obedient to Christ, He will draw the kids He wants to Himself.

One year we had 240 kids at Club every week all semester. We had four leaders and about fifty Campaigner kids. I didn't know what the next week would bring. I didn't know what the next year would bring. I only knew that God had richly blessed our commitment to investing our lives into the lives of Campaigner kids and we were having a great time seeing so many kids come to club.

Paul tells the church in Thessalonica, 1 Thessalonians 2:19–20, "For what is our hope or joy or crown of boasting before our Lord Jesus at His coming? Is it not you? For you are our glory and our joy." Our job as ministers, as servants of God's Word, is to give our lives to other people. Paul tells us that our joy before the Lord—our crown of boasting before the Lord—is those whom we have given our lives to. God does not call us to run a great program. God calls us to invest our lives in people.

For years I was petrified of roller coasters. I would stand under the great wooden structures, look up at the rattling and shaking, and my stomach would sink with fear. When I was twenty-three years old, a group of high school kids shamed me into riding a roller coaster with them. It was thrilling and exhilarating. The feeling of tension and anxiety as the roller coaster cars climbed to the heights, the feeling of being out of control as I lost my stomach on the downward slope and shoot back up only to be thrust downward again was fantastic. That day I rode the roller coaster three times. There are two ways to ride a roller coaster. The first way—which isn't much fun—is to grab the safety bar and hold on as tightly as you can, just enduring the ride until it's over. The second—and best—way to ride a roller coaster is to put your hands in the air, scream the entire time, and love every minute of it.

The real thrill of being a Christian is when we "put our hands in the air" and risk ourselves to do those things of which we are afraid. We go to contacts and are afraid of rejection, but God meets us there and a kid says, "Hi," and we are thrilled. We go to Club, and we are sweating bullets all day worrying about how it's going to go. Then kids come and it's great fun, and we sense God's power in our lives. We have met our fears and gotten on God's roller coaster. He has taken us to the heights and given us the thrills we would not otherwise have known.

The essence of this book is that we would not ride the roller coaster alone, but we would instead take kids along for the greatest ride of life itself—a ride through life with Christ. My conclusion is that as Christian kids give themselves to other people, they will see Christ work in their lives, and when they experience Christ working in their lives, it will be the best thing for their spiritual growth as well as for the growth of the Kingdom. As I have watched kids give their lives to Christ and then commit themselves to reaching out in their school for Christ, I see in their faces and their lives the joy of knowing what it is to have God meet them at their fears. That joy becomes a foundation for a life of fruitful obedience to Christ.

My desire for all who read this book is that they might take God's principles of giving their lives to Christ and to others and share that great thrill with the kids they are privileged to work with. In the end, we will all say with Paul, "What is our hope or joy or crown of boasting at His coming, is it not you, for you are our glory and our joy" (1 Thessalonians. 2:19–20).

 Final Thoughts

The End in Mind

In the beginning of this book I wrote about "beginning with the end in mind." I recently celebrated my sixtieth birthday and it was perhaps the greatest birthday celebration anyone could ever have. The weeklong festivities began with a party on Saturday night with my peers—friends that I have known for most of those sixty years—that was a wonderful celebration. My best friend from high school came, my best friend from college came, friends from my Baltimore years, Bethlehem years, St Louis years, Canadian years and a large group of friends in Philadelphia, all turned out for a fabulous party that my wonderful wife put together at our house.

The next weekend my best friend Eric gathered "my guys" for dinner at a wonderful private club in Philadelphia. Eric was one of the "All Stars" in the Bethlehem club that I've written about in this book. Twenty-seven guys who were the

"All Stars" in every area I lived gathered for an unforgettable evening. They came from all over - Vancouver, Los Angeles, Puerto Rico, Toronto, Colorado, St Louis, Raleigh, and Philadelphia—to be together for that one night. Not all had been in my Young Life club. Some were guys I met after I left Young Life staff, and I was no longer leading club. Nonetheless, they were guys I believed the Lord was leading me to invest in and I had the privilege of connecting with and sharing faith and life with.

In one evening there was a glimpse of what it looks like when you "begin with the end in mind." Some of the guys are still in the full time ministry; most are not. Many have gone on to highly successful careers and are contributing to their churches and communities as men of God. All are continuing to be God's men in this broken world. They are Christian husbands, fathers and co-workers. They are leaders and are being used by God in this world.

As I looked around the table I thought of the great privilege I had to know and love each of them. Each guy, each story, each relationship was a gift and a blessing, and it was my privilege to have been able to know and love them. I also thought of how, at the time, it didn't seem like it was a very big impact. It was only a couple of guys at any one point in time, and sometimes I wondered if following the disciple model of Jesus would be worth it. There was always so much pressure to give in to the banana split, and I was always fighting to not do the gimmicks. Now, looking back over forty years of investing in people—looking around that table - it has in fact been quite a huge impact. It is the kind of impact you never get from a hundred foot banana split. It is the kind of impact you only get from rejecting the "passing parade" mentality and focusing instead on deeply loving people.

That night gave me a renewed sense of energy for investing in more men for the remaining years of my life. Not that I would build God's Kingdom for Him, but that through His grace, He would allow me the privilege of loving people as He builds His Kingdom through me.

ᴄᵃ⫘Appendix Aᴼᴼ⫘

THE TWENTY-THREE THINGS CAMPAIGNERS DO
THE DAY OF CLUB

Many years ago, I realized that part of my frustration with Campaigners was due to my lack of communicating to them exactly what I expected of them. As a result, I developed this list of "The Twenty-Three Things Campaigners Do the Day of Club." I hope this is as helpful for you as it has been for our folks.

BEFORE CLUB

1. Pray First Thing in The Morning: Before our feet hit the floor, we should pray. While we're in the shower, while eating breakfast, on the way to school—whenever or wherever be committed to prayer. Nothing great has ever been accomplished except by prayer. Hudson Taylor's great quote

was, "Move men by God through prayer alone." Club day is a holy day, and it must be immersed in prayer.

2. Invite Friends to Club: We are about relational evangelism, and there should be investment of life upon life in our ministry. Therefore, as we give ourselves to Campaigner kids, we must help them give themselves to their friends. This builds a healthy view of relational ministry and of giving themselves to their friends (1 Thess. 2:8). It helps them not rely on "programs" or "gimmicks" but enables them to be incarnational witnesses. It also creates "kid ownership."

3. Fill Car With Non-Christian Friends: We are not interested in carloads of Christian kids at Club. Club is for non-Christians. Campaigner cliques can kill a Club.

CLUB

4. Stay with the Friends You Brought and Make Them Feel Comfortable: One sure way to have people come once and never come back again is to have them dropped at Club by the person who brought them while that person hangs around with their other friends. They will feel used and uncared for. On the other hand, a person who feels accepted and cared for will return week after week.

5. Make Club Fun: Club involves kids, and it is not a show from up front where the leader does the entertaining. Many times I've had Campaigners who looked at me as if to say, "So what are you going to do to entertain me?" It is their Club, and they are equally responsible for making it "happen."

6. Don't Sit with Other Campaigners: This correlates with number 4 in this list. The ugliest sight at a Young Life Club is little groups of Campaigners sitting together and ignoring the

rest of the Club. Even if they didn't bring anyone else themselves, they should help with others who did.

7. Everybody Sings: Everyone wants to be cool and they are afraid to sing, because they are afraid that someone might think they're not cool. This is particularly true of guys. They need to trust this tool of Young Life Club and realize that in the same way they have fun singing, others will also if they will take the lead and risk themselves.

8. Get People around You to Sing: It is not enough for Campaigners to sing themselves, but it is important that they encourage others around them to get into the singing. This is especially true for those people they brought.

9. Be Rowdy during Rowdy Songs,- Even When No One Else Is: Sometimes when Club starts off slow, or it is a tough room in which to get things going, Campaigners have to work extra hard to make those fast songs work.

10. Don't Yell Out Wrong Timed Songs. There always seems to be someone who wants to sing their favorite slow song at the beginning of Club or their favorite fast song at the end of Club. Songs are structured the way they are (fast songs first, slow songs after Minutes) in order to set up the talk. To break that order is to damage the proclamation. The music at the end of the slow songs should prepare their hearts to hear the message.

11. Sing Slow Songs: Don't Talk–Sing: Because the slow songs have a message, and can create an atmosphere where serious things can be discussed, there is a tendency among Campaigners to feel uneasy. They often will talk to the friends they brought, hoping to distract them from the change in mood of Club. They need to understand the importance of these

transitional songs and that as they model interest in them, they actually help their friends prepare for the message. They also need to trust the Holy Spirit to begin working in them. Many kids will remember the lyrics and tune of a spiritual song long after they have forgotten the talk. God will use these songs to prepare their hearts.

12. Cheer for Minutes and the People Who Are in It: We really need Campaigners to help with the enthusiasm of Minutes. Sometimes a given Minutes can drag, and this is where Campaigner kids can keep the thing from being a disaster. It is also important for them to recognize when one person or team is being cheered for by the whole Club, while the other person or team is being ignored by the whole Club. This is when Campaigners should make sure the other team or person is cheered for also.

13. Shut Up during the Talk: I know that sounds harsh, but the single most annoying thing Campaigners do is talk to others during the talk. They may have heard the talk before; in fact, I hope they have. They may know exactly where I am going when I talk; I hope they do. When they talk, they distract others who may have never heard the talk before and need to hear it. This may be a function of their insecurities. Sometimes they are afraid that their friends will not like the talk or any conversation about God. We need to encourage them to trust God, which can be a cutting edge issue for many of them.

14. Pray for the Speaker: The thing I want my Campaigners to do most of all during the talk is pray. I know that we are fighting a spiritual war and the primary weapon is prayer. It has been a great joy to me to be able to look out on Club and know there are kids praying for me as I speak.

15. Help Others Be Quiet: If there are those around who want to talk during the talk, it is helpful for Campaigners to ask them to be quiet so the leader doesn't have to make a big deal of it. It is only a set up for failure for the leader to have to say something from up front when a peer can take care of it from the floor.

AFTER CLUB

16. Introduce Friends to Leaders: It is important for new kids to meet the leader so that they feel they have some rapport with the person in charge of this whole thing. More importantly, the leader should meet the new kids at Club. If the leader is going to be praying for these kids and talking to them in the future (at school, contacts, or wherever), an introduction by someone else is very helpful. This also promotes a sense of belonging for the new person.

17. Meet All New People There: It is not only important for the new people to meet the leader, it is important for them to meet the other kids in Club, especially the Campaigners. Each Campaigner should be aware of the new people and meet them, as well as make sure that the people they brought meet other Campaigners.

18. Drive (or Go with) Friends You Brought to McDonalds (or wherever You Go After Club): Campaigners need to realize that they have brought people for the entire evening, and the night is not over when Club ends. There is nothing worse than someone feeling dumped after Club is over. I have seen incidents where new non-Christian kids came up to meet me after Club and asked me for a ride to McDonalds or home because the person who brought them left them behind.

19. Drive Safely: It is not our job to parent or police the kids who come to Club, but if kids die in car accidents on the way to or from Club, it could wipe us out (to say nothing of the eternal consequences). Parents will be reluctant to allow their kids to be a part of Club if they think that their kids' lives are in danger. Campaigners must have this impressed upon them, because as they try to cover their insecurities and prove to their friends how cool they are, they endanger the lives of their friends.

20. Take (or Go with) the People You Brought Home: This is similar to number 18 and just as important. It is a terrible feeling to be left alone at McDonalds looking for a ride or having to call your parents. Campaigners should make sure everyone has a ride home. They are especially responsible for the people they bring.

21. Ask for Feedback When Possible: Campaigners should look for ways to ask what their friends thought of Club, the talk, the people, the leaders, the songs, the Minutes, etc. This feedback is very valuable to the future of the Club and it is helpful to the leader. It also makes the person feel that his or her input is valuable. Most importantly, however, Campaigners should be looking for opportunities to follow up the talk and share Christ with their friends.

22. Care: In everything we do, we should communicate that we really care about kids as people, not as just another number at our deal. We are about people meeting Christ, and our compassion for them must be the single most important thing they remember. I know that kids will remember very little of what I say but a lot of who I am. "More is caught than taught."

23. Pray and Thank God for the Evening: No matter how Club goes, who comes, or who doesn't come, we should thank God for the evening. Sometimes it is difficult when things don't go the way we want them to, but we must realize that it is God's club and we are His servants. We are fortunate to be so. The last thing we should do before going to bed that night is thank the Lord for what He is accomplishing through us and the great things He is doing. We have a whole week to make our petitions to the Lord for the next Club, we should take this time right after Club to just be still before the Lord and be thankful.

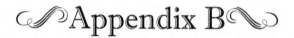Appendix B

PRINCIPLES FOR STUDYING THE BIBLE

INTRODUCTION:

Perhaps the most important thing we can do as Christians is to study and understand the Bible. The Bible is God's revelation to us of His nature, will, and sovereignty over all of creation. While it contains several different genre (poetic, historical, philosophical) each passage of Scripture is a revelation of God. It is our joy and refreshment to study His Word and participate in His revelation. As we understand His Word, we grow in our communion with Him, and the joy of our salvation is increased as we see His loving hand holding every inch of the universe in His sovereign will.

Sadly, we live in an age where most people—even professional Christian workers—are without the essential skills of understanding the Bible. We live in a culture that is

Biblically illiterate. As we seek to lead and disciple those whom God brings to our ministry, we must learn to accurately teach God's Word to the next generation of believers. If we are the primary teacher of God's truth to new believers, it becomes even more important for us to be well equipped at teaching the truth of God's Word. Unfortunately, most of us have not experienced solid Biblical teaching ourselves, and therefore it is even more difficult for us to teach the Word to others. In the following pages, I hope to outline some basic principles that will guide you in your own study of God's Word.

Principle # 1: The God/Christ-Centeredness of Every Passage of Scripture.

The first and most important principle of studying the Bible is to look for the "God/Christ-Centeredness" of each passage. We must remember that the Bible is about God, and is His revelation to us of His design, plan, and sovereign will. In our culture, we tend to be self-consumed and think that everything in life is about us. To rephrase the old Carly Simon song, "We're so vain, we probably think the Bible's about us," but it's not—it's about God.

In each passage, therefore, we should look to see how the particular story, event, or teaching is about God. What is He doing? What is He teaching? How is this about Him, His sovereignty, and His revelation of His glory?

Several years ago, I was in France with my family, and we were visiting the Cathedral at Chartres. In a semicircle surrounding the nave of the cathedral and facing outward are a series of reliefs cut in stone, depicting various events in the life of Jesus. It begins with His birth and proceeds through His various miracles and healings to His death, resurrection, and ascension. As I stood looking at them with my two sons, I was asking them what story each relief told. They stared at the cold stone and had no idea as we moved from one ancient sculpture to the next.

Then an idea hit me. I asked them to see if they could identify Jesus in the relief. In just a few seconds, they could identify Him. Then I asked if they could identify the rest of the story once they knew which character was Jesus and what he was doing. Almost instantly they were able to say, "Feeding the five thousand," or "Calming the sea." When they focused on Jesus, they were able to get the right meaning from the art.

The entire Bible is like this for us. We must focus on Christ and what He is doing if we are going to understand the true meaning of any given passage.

There is a funny thing about this exercise. Once you start seeing the "Christ-Centeredness" of each passage, you won't be able to "unsee" it. You will wonder how you ever missed it before, and it will begin to jump out at you. For some reason, we haven't been trained to think this way, but when we do, the obviousness of it is overwhelming.

One example of how we miss this is in the story of Zacchaeus in Luke 19. You remember Zacchaeus. He was a short tax collector. His neighbors disliked him and he climbed up into a sycamore tree to see Jesus. We have probably all heard that this story is about Zacchaeus and how if we will be like him—get in a place where we can see Jesus—then He will come to our house and we can be saved.

This sounds so good to our needy ears. We want to hear how the Bible is about us and what we can do to have God love us. We want to know what we can do to be in control. But it misses so much of the text, and this interpretation invites other problems of interpretation.

For starters, there were many other people in the crowd that day who saw Jesus, but He didn't go to any of their homes. If this story is about getting to a place where we can see Jesus, then why didn't it apply to the many people who were along the side of the road looking at Jesus? More importantly, to understand this event in terms of how it applies to us is to miss the meaning of the last verse, the one where Jesus actually speaks and gives the meaning to the story.

In Luke 19:9-10 Jesus says, "Today salvation has come to this house, because he also is a son of Abraham; for the Son of man has come to seek and to save that which is lost." Jesus tells us that his encounter with Zacchaeus illustrates that He has come to seek and to save lost people. Jesus seeks out lost people and Jesus saves them. That is the message of the event—at least it is the message Jesus tells us about the event.

Now let's look at this passage again from the perspective of the interpretation Jesus gives us in those last two verses. When Jesus entered the town, He knew Zacchaeus's name. He called to him up in the tree and told him to come down, that He must go to his house for dinner. Jesus, not Zacchaeus initiated the conversation. Jesus called him by name—which he knew before he entered the town— and Jesus pursued him, not the other way around. Does anyone think that if Zacchaeus weren't up in the tree Jesus would have missed him? Is it possible that Jesus—the One who created the universe, knows all things, and is in control of all things—wouldn't have been able to find Zacchaeus if he wasn't up in the tree? Of course not. Then why do we put so much emphasis on Zacchaeus going up in the tree? It's colorful and adds to the man-centeredness of the story, but it is unessential to the point of the story. This story is about Jesus and how He seeks after bad people (the worst guy in town) and He saves them.

What about Zacchaeus offering to give away half of what he has stolen? Doesn't this denote that we must act before we are saved? Note that this reparation on the part of Zacchaeus is a response to Jesus already being in his house, it is not a prerequisite to Jesus's visit. Jesus doesn't say to him, "If you repay damages, then I'll come to your house," He says, "I'm coming to your house." That's it. No strings. No requirements. No quid pro quo. Jesus comes and Zacchaeus responds. That's what happens, and Jesus interprets it for us. He comes to seek and to save the lost. This passage also illustrates principle number 2.

EXERCISES FOR FURTHER STUDY:

Read Psalm 23, noticing the pronouns used by David. How is this Christ/God-Centered?

Read Nehemiah 1–2. How is this passage about God (notice particularly verses 2:12, 18, and 20)?

PRINCIPLE # 2: THE BIBLE IS THE BEST COMMENTARY ON THE BIBLE.

When Jesus or another Biblical author tells us the meaning of a particular event or parable, we need to understand that this is the intended meaning. Jesus tells us that the point of the encounter with Zacchaeus is to illustrate that He seeks people, and He saves them. This happens often in the Scripture—more often than we notice—and we need to make sure that we understand the Bible in accordance with what is intended to be taught.

Another example of this is in the parable of the Pharisee and the tax collector in Luke 18. We must first note that this is a parable. A parable is a story told for the purpose of illustrating a specific point (or points), and it's very important that we understand the right point (or points) of the story. In this particular parable, the point is that some people trust in themselves to be saved, but they are missing the Gospel. The Bible tells us this in the first verse, Luke 18:9, "Also He spoke this parable to some who trusted in themselves that they were righteous, and despised others..." These are the points of the parable—that we are not to trust in ourselves for salvation, and we are not to despise others.

We must be careful with parables not to make them into more than they carry. We are not to "squeeze" out of a parable more than it is intended to teach. For example, in the parable of the prodigal son, we often hear well-meaning speakers embellish the story to make more than one point. But in that parable, the point is clear: we are not to resent those whom the Father forgives. We know this because of the third principle.

PRINCIPLE # 3: "CONTEXT IS YOUR FRIEND."

In the parable of the prodigal son, we can look to whom it is being told, and where it fits alongside the other parables that precede it and see the context. This parable comes in Luke 15:11–32. Luke 15:1–3 shows us the audience to which each of the next three parables are told, "Then all the tax collectors and the sinners drew near to Him to hear Him. And the Pharisees and scribes complained, saying, 'This Man receives sinners and eats with them. So He spoke this parable to them saying…'"

Here Luke gives us the setting—crowds of tax collectors and sinners drawing near to Jesus, and the audience the parables are directed toward, complaining Pharisees and scribes—and tells us that Jesus was using these three parables to answer the complaints of the Pharisees and scribes. Then two parables are told to illustrate the point that God searches after lost people in the same way that humans search after a lost sheep or lost coins. In each of these two parables, Jesus gives us the interpretation of the parable. In Luke 15:7, Jesus gives us the meaning of the lost coin. He says, "I say to you that likewise there will be more joy in heaven over one sinner who repents than over ninety-nine just persons who need no repentance." In Luke 15:10, Jesus gives us the meaning of the parable of the lost coin. He says, "Likewise, I say to you, there is joy in the presence of the angels of God over one sinner who repents." These two parables and their interpretation along with the audience of Pharisees and scribes give us the context in the parable of the lost son. These two parables set the groundwork for the revolutionary teaching he will give to the Pharisees and scribes in the final parable.

The parable of the lost son is similar to the preceding two parables in that it teaches the forgiveness of the father, but this parable goes further. In this parable, Jesus adds the character of the older brother. The older brother represents the audience Jesus is speaking to, the complaining scribes and Pharisees. The older son is the one who is angry that the father has accepted his younger brother when he returns home. Jesus is telling the Pharisees that the father accepts with joy those who were lost but now are found, which is consistent with the message of the previous two parables.

119

The additional, special emphasis Jesus puts on the parable of the lost son is in the wrong attitude of the older brother. He is aiming this parable at the scribes and Pharisees and telling them that they have the wrong attitude toward the sinners He receives and eats with. He is telling this parable to refute the complaints of the Pharisees and scribes.

Sometimes, even when Jesus interprets the parable for us we still get it wrong. This brings us to principle number four.

PRINCIPLE # 4: KNOW THE DIFFERENCE BETWEEN DESCRIPTIVE AND PRESCRIPTIVE.

Remember I said earlier that we want the Bible to be about us? Perhaps you've heard it said that the Bible is God's "owner's manual" of how we're to live. Well, yes and no. God does tell us how He wants us to live, but it's not our owner's manual, it's God's! God is sharing with us His "owner's manual" and telling us how He lives. He lives. He Lives. HE LIVES. YES, HE LIVES!

With this in mind, we need to understand that much of the scripture is God describing His world, His creation, His plan, His will, and His ways, not prescribing for us a specific mode of action. We see this clearly in the parable of the sower or, more accurately, the parable of the soils in Matthew 12:1–9 and Mark 4:1–12.

In this parable, Jesus is describing for us the various responses to the Word of God. The disciples question Him later, and He explains the parable by telling them in detail what each seed/soil combination represents. The illustration is clear that the seed is the Word of God and people are the receivers of the seed, the soil.

In this parable, Jesus is describing what happens to the seed when it is strewn into different soils. He is describing what happens to the seed. He is not prescribing any action on the part of the soils. In fact, if we understand our part in the parable as being the "dirt," then we can see that dirt is a fairly inactive substance. It's not working hard at being dirt; it's not trying to be better dirt. It is simply what it was from the beginning of time. Dirt![ix]

Yet we often hear that we are the sowers in the parable and we must therefore go out and sow on good soil. Or perhaps we've heard it said that we must be the good soil, and we must work hard to produce fruit in order to be good soil. In either case, we are in danger of contorting the parable to make it say something Jesus never intended it to mean. We are making it prescriptive—attempting to make it prescribe an action to us—when it is in fact a descriptive parable. The problem here, of course is that we are always desperate for how the Bible applies to our lives. We're always looking for an application—and application is important—and that leads us to principle number five.

PRINCIPLE # 5: NINETY PERCENT OF HERESY OCCURS IN APPLICATION.

It's not just bad interpretation to tell people they must work at being "good soil," or that they must work to sow the Word on good soil, or that they must get in a tree to see Jesus, or that the Bible is their "owner's manual," it is heresy. When we make the Gospel about adding "laws" or "works" to the grace of God, we are perverting the Gospel of grace, which is God's free gift, and making it into a work of ours. As Bryan

Chapell, president of Covenant Seminary has said, "Legalism is not sub-Gospel, it's anti-Gospel."

We're not dealing with trivial things here. This is not the same as dealing with the allegorical meanings of "The Old Man and the Sea" or some other human writing. We're dealing with the revealed Word of God, and it is incumbent upon us to focus on Him and make sure our applications are to His glory. In other words, it's important to get it right; it's important to get the application right.

We live in a Biblically illiterate culture, and we must bring the truth as it is revealed in the Scripture to this culture in order to educate them in the truth of God's plan and will. This is important business, and we must not take it lightly. The application of God's truth is very important, and we must work to make sure we understand what God's Word is calling us to do.

I was in a men's group that was studying 1 Samuel. In this group, we looked at a chapter each week and then talked about what God was doing and how it applied to our lives. As we were studying chapter 16 (Samuel being led by God to discern God's choice for the future king), we came upon the familiar verse, 1 Samuel 16:7, "But the Lord said to Samuel, 'Do not look at his appearance or at his physical stature, because I have refused him. For the Lord does not see as man sees; for man looks at the outward appearance, but the Lord looks at the heart.'"

Our group raced immediately to what seemed like the appropriate application. If God looks on the inside then we should also. But as I thought about that verse and its context (God choosing His king), I was struck by the thought that we're not God. The true application seems to be quite the opposite of what is common. God looks on the inside and we can't. What happens when we try to look on the inside of other people? Well, for starters we can't, so we more often than not get it wrong. Second, we become judgmental of others. Third, we make assumptions based on what we suppose and those assumptions are more often than not wrong. To think that this verse is instructing us to look on the inside of other people is the wrong application. The right application is that only God can look on the inside, and we must trust Him to do so.

Here the Bible is not instructing us to look on the inside of other people—something we can't do—but rather to understand that it is only God who can look on the inside of any of us. Even Samuel, the great prophet of God, was unable to look on the inside of the young David to see that he was God's chosen instrument to be His king. This leads us to the next principle.

PRINCIPLE #6: STUDY PASSAGES NOT VERSES.

The curse of studying verses instead of passages is the common practice known as "proof-texting," and it is dangerous at best. You know you can string together a set of verses to make the Bible say most anything you want it to say. Nowadays when I hear a speaker quote a verse, I usually look up that verse to see the context of the entire passage before I allow myself to buy into the point he is making. Too many people have used proof-texting to make the Bible say all kinds of crazy things.

Here is an absurd example. Take the verse "and Judas went and hanged himself" and couple it with "go ye and do likewise" and you have the basis for a completely blasphemous sermon. Of course no one would preach that sermon, but it is not much better to tell people through proof-texting that they need to be good in order to enter heaven, that they need to have quiet times every day, that the family is the most important thing in life, or any number of current bad teachings.

The Scripture was written as complete thoughts, and we must look at the entire "thought passage" in order to get the whole and true meaning of the passage. This is particularly true with the Pauline Epistles. When Paul makes a point, he almost always does it in the context of a long and developed thought. He is logical and rational, and his thought process builds from one point to the next. His letters are not a series of disjointed "sayings" that are helpful for everyday living (See point number 1: the Bible is not about you.) but rather a logical progression of thoughts that build on each other and come to deep spiritual conclusions.

For example, one of Paul's most quoted phrases is also one of his most abused thoughts when taken out of context and placed alone on the tray of trite chrisitanese. In Paul's brilliant letter to the church in Rome, he says in chapter 8, verse 28, "And we know that all things work together for good to those who love God, to those who are the called according to His purpose." As wonderful and reassuring as this verse is, we must understand the whole context of this verse and where it comes in the entire letter.

This verse applies to Christians. Paul is not saying that everything will work together for good for non-Christians. In fact, it is not going to end well for them at all. It's going to be bad for them. Paul is telling Christians that because God foreknew and predestined them to be conformed to the image of His Son, all things will work together for good for them. To take this verse out of the context of the larger passage is to miss the point of the verse and in fact give false guidance to those who may be led to believe that even as nonbelievers things will work out for them.

Let's take another example from Paul in Galatians 3:28 where he writes, "There is neither Jew nor Greek, there is neither slave nor free, there is neither male nor female; for you are all one in Christ Jesus." This is a great thought in the midst of Paul explaining the equality of believers with regard to salvation. He has just made his case for the purpose of the law (3:19–23) and is now moving on to introduce the idea of adoption as sons by God (4:4–7). In this line of thought, Paul is saying that we are all adopted as sons (and not sons and daughters, since Paul is saying that both male and female will be regarded in the culturally esteemed place of the Son) and are therefore equal in our standing with the Father for salvific purposes.

This verse has nothing to do with church offices or the positions that can be held in the church by either men or women. It is a misuse of the verse to make it say something that it does not say, yet I have heard this verse used many times to make a case for the ordination of women. I'm not even saying that case can't be made from other sections of Scripture, but I am saying that this verse taken in its complete context does not address that issue at all.

One more example. Let's look at the familiar verse often used to prescribe conversion in Revelation 3:20 which says, "Behold, I stand at the door and knock. If anyone hears My voice and opens the door, I will come in to him and dine with him, and he with Me."

Again, we must look at the whole section and not just this verse to get the true meaning. John's revelation is a prophetic warning to the church. Jesus is speaking through John to Christians. Before He tells them to open the doors of their hearts and let Him be Lord, He is warning them to repent of their luke warmness and their dependence on themselves (vs 17–18) and that the ones He loves He rebukes (vs 19). This is His promise to the Christians of Laodicea and not a formula for conversion, yet it has been taken out of context to be so.

We are too anxious to pull a verse out of context to make the Bible say what we want it to. Often we think about what we want to say and then go searching the Scripture for a verse to back it up. Instead we need to let the text speak to us and then teach what it says, not what we want it to say.

This is the more difficult approach, because it requires us to study the entire passage, understand the background, and grasp the context. Sometimes the God/Christ-Centeredness is not immediately apparent, and we have to think and study hard to see it. Sometimes the application is not immediately obvious, but we have to let the Holy Spirit speak to us and hear the true application. This is the work of the Bible teacher or preacher. It is our job to study the Word and accurately teach and preach it to others. And this leads us to the next principle.

PRINCIPLE # 7: THE VERSE YOU DON'T THINK MAKES SENSE IS PROBABLY THE KEY TO RE-UNDERSTANDING THE ENTIRE PASSAGE.

Sometimes there is a verse in a passage that doesn't seem to fit. It doesn't go with the flow of how we understand the rest of the passage. We think we've got the meaning, but there is that one verse that just doesn't seem to make sense. Take for example the great poetic string of couplets in 2 Timothy 2:11–13. Here Paul says, "This is a faithful saying: For if we died with Him we shall also live with Him. If we endure, we shall also reign with Him. If we deny Him, He also will deny us. If we are faithless He remains faithful; He cannot deny Himself."

We want to say, "What? Paul, this is a great thought right up until the end. It makes sense that if we die with Him, we'll live with Him, and if we endure we'll reign, and if we deny Him He'll deny us. But if we're faithless you should also be saying that He will be faithless to us also. You've got it wrong, Paul. You made a mistake. You said "He remains faithful because He cannot deny Himself."

The key to understanding this is to re-understand the verse that doesn't seem to fit. Jesus is always faithful to us, because we are His creation, His workmanship, His sons. Even when we're faithless—and we're a lot more faithless than we are faithful—He remains faithful, because He cannot deny His own workmanship, His own creation.

Another example is in the parable of the persistent widow in Luke 18. After Jesus tells the parable, encouraging us to pray without ceasing, He includes the last verse. Luke 18:8 says, "Nevertheless, when the Son of Man comes, will He really find faith on earth?" This is one of those verses we skip over quickly because we think we've already got the point of the parable, but the real, deeper meaning lies here. While Jesus is encouraging us to pray without ceasing, He's also telling us that faith—trusting God—is the thing that He desires in our prayers. This then, leads us to our next point.

PRINCIPLE # 8: THE BIBLE IS NOT SIMPLISTIC.

We live in an age of simplicity. It seems that the goal of modern consumerism is to make our lives simpler. How many times have I fought for a parking spot just ten feet closer to the mall so I won't have to walk that extra ten feet? Or how often do I look at the microwave and think it's taking too long to cook things. This is the culture we live in. We want things simple and fast, and we don't have much tolerance for that which is complex and takes time.

We get in a lot of trouble when we reduce the Bible to quick and simple sound bites or easy "rules to live by." Much of what the Bible teaches is complex and takes thought and wisdom to understand. Some things are clear and are taught clearly in the Bible. The Ten Commandments aren't the Ten Suggestions. They are clear and they are what God has set out as His perfect law. But there is much that isn't clear, and we need to be able to navigate the Scripture through the parameters that are outlined.

Take for example the relatively easy issue of prayer. Jesus tells us through the parable of the persistent widow in Luke 18 that we "always ought to pray and not lose heart." When the elders of Israel demanded a king of God, it seems like they were acting just like Jesus is telling us to act in the parable. They wanted a King and they were demanding one of God. Instead, they are said to be rejecting God. 1 Samuel 8:7 says, "And the Lord said to Samuel, 'Heed the voice of the people in all that they say to you; for they have not rejected you, but they have rejected Me, that I should not reign over them.'"

How then are we to pray? Are we to be like the persistent widow or like the elders? Where is the right perspective for our prayers?

Or how about social issues like alcohol? Jesus's first miracle is turning water into wine, and Paul instructs young Timothy to drink wine for his stomach. Yet Paul also warns us not to be drunk with wine. Take Psalm 104:15, which gives praise to God for "wine that makes glad the heart of man" and Proverbs 20:1 which says, "Wine is a mocker." How do we fit these things together so that we are neither legalists nor drunkards? Simplistic answers and formulas won't do here. We must provide wisdom, discernment, and understanding to navigate these waters and give instruction to others on the way.

How will we handle issues like ordaining women, baptism, predestination, homosexuality, or a plethora of other issues that the Bible speaks of? We cannot respond in a simplistic form that fits conveniently into our modern world, where quick answers, thirty second commercials and five-second sound bites are the norm. We must offer a reasoned and mature response that enables the believer to have a solid foundation for his/her thinking.

How will the truth of God revealed in the Bible lead and direct our lives to His glory if we are unable or unwilling to give His Word the deep thought and meditation it requires? John Calvin said, "The Bible is a lot bigger than your favorite parts," and we need to have an understanding of the whole counsel of the Scripture in order for us to put its teachings in the context of the total revelation of God. This of course leads us to the next principle.

PRINCIPLE #9: DON'T RUN AWAY FROM PROBLEMS IN THE PASSAGE.

What do you do with "problem" passages? These are the passages that don't fit neatly into your particular theological construct. It seems that most of us simply skip over these difficult verses to get to our favorite parts.

Take for example the difficult passage in 1 Samuel 16, just after Samuel has found and anointed David as King. 1 Samuel 16:14 says, "But the Spirit of the Lord departed from Saul, and an evil spirit from the Lord troubled him." Does God send evil spirits to trouble people? I don't know about you, but this is a difficult verse for me to deal with. What does it say about God or rather my understanding of Him? What am I to do with this verse?

Or how about the entire chapter of 2 Samuel 24? Here David is led to number the people of Israel, condemned for his sin, and seventy thousand Israelites are killed by God as a result. Is this not a difficult passage? It gets even more difficult when you consider that the same event recorded in 1 Chronicles 21 says that it was Satan who moved David to number the people. What are we to do with these difficult passages?

How about Paul's teaching on not allowing women to have authority over men in 1 Timothy 2:11–15? What are we to make of this? Do we throw it out because our contemporary culture has changed, or do we hold to a literal view that is clearly oppressive to women in church leadership? What do we do with these kinds of difficult verses?

I have one suggestion: It's OK to not understand everything about the Bible, God, or the Christian faith. It's OK because we're not God. It is always a comfort to me to come upon those things in the Bible that I have no clue about and realize that the God of the Bible—the one who created the universe, sent Jesus to die and rise from the dead, and who will return this all to His ultimate glory—is bigger than my comprehension. That is a good thing, a comforting thought. When I get to those passages, I am free to simply say, "I don't know." This leads us to the final principle.

PRINCIPLE #10: LOGICAL IS NOT NECESSARILY THEOLOGICAL.

Another key to understanding the Scriptures, especially the difficult parts, is to understand that "logical is not necessarily theological." For example, when Jesus turns water into wine, heals a paralytic, walks on water, or raises Lazarus from the dead, it's certainly not logical. But all of these events are deeply theological, because they are an outworking of God having become a man. Jesus supersedes logic because He is outside of our logical realm. There is no logic in miracles, only the working of God who is outside of our time and space; and that too is a good thing. If miracles were logical, they wouldn't be miracles.

This principle also applies to theological tenets that are not miracles. It is not logical that God would choose an individual (Abraham) and make a chosen nation from him. It's not logical that God's chosen nation would suffer and be persecuted for their entire existence. It's not logical that God would choose people before the beginning of time to be His and redeem those people through His Son's death and resurrection. These theological events aren't logical to our human understanding, but they are deeply theological as they are the will of God.

We must be careful not to make God fit into our box and fit into a picture of what we think He should be and how He should act. If He wants to build a nation from Abraham or send an evil spirit to Saul, or choose people for salvation, that is His prerogative. It's not necessarily logical, but it is deeply theological.

This list is not, of course, exhaustive, but I hope it will serve as a beginning of deeper thought as you look at the Scriptures and teach it to others.

∝Appendix C∞

Below is the statistical summary of the various areas where I served and applied the "No Banana Splits" model of ministry. I provide this list here only because some may question the effectiveness of the model, and I do so with all humility knowing that God is the provider of all things—especially the numbers.

BALTIMORE, MARYLAND, VOLUNTEER, Dulaney High School, 1979–1981

Started Club with 5 sophomore girls. The Club grew to over 120 every week within one year.

BETHLEHEM, PENNSYLVANIA, 1992–1987

WORK WITH KIDS:

Number of Clubs grew from 1 to 7.
Number of kids in Clubs each week grew from 15 to 350.
Number of kids in Campaigners grew from 0 to 115.

Volunteer leaders:

The number of volunteer leaders group from 5 to 35.

Funding:

The financial base grew from $60,000 to $120,000.

St. Louis, Missouri, 1987–1996

Work with kids:

Number of Clubs grew from 2 to 6.
Number of kids in Clubs each week grew from 100 to 620.
Number of kids in Campaigners grew from 10 to 160.

Volunteer leaders:

The number of volunteer leaders grew from 4 to 20.

Staff:

The number of staff grew from 1 staff person to 2 full-time and 3 part-time staff.

Funding:

The financial base grew from $80,000 to $250,000.

Ontario, Canada, 1996–2003

Work with kids:

Number of Clubs grew 0 to 7.

Number of kids in Clubs each week grew from 0 to 210.
Number of kids in Campaigners grew from 0 to 50 each week.

Staff:

The number of staff grew from 2 full-time to 6 full-time staff.

Funding:

The financial base grew from $80,000 to almost $800,000.

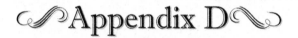Appendix D

My Typical Weekly Schedule as an Area Director

Sunday

Morning: Teach Sunday School

Church

Evening: Adult Bible Study Group

Monday

Morning: Office

Lunch: Donor/Leader

Afternoon: Office

Afternoon: Contacts

Tuesday

Morning: Office

Lunch: Donor/Leader

Afternoon: Office

Afternoon: Contacts (spring & fall)

Evening: Contacts (winter)

Wednesday

Morning: Office

Lunch: Donor/Leader

Afternoon: Club prep

Evening: Club

Thursday

Morning: Office

Lunch: Donor/Leader

Afternoon: Office

Afternoon: Contacts

Friday

Early Morning: Campaigners

Lunch: Donor/Leader

Afternoon: Office

Evening: Contacts

Saturday:

Evening: Leadership (once a month Committee)

✐About the Author✐

B ob Perkins served on the staff of Young Life from 1982 to 2004, first in Bethlehem, Pennsylvania, (1982-1997), then in St. Louis,

Missouri, (1987-1996), and finally with Young Life Canada as Provincial Director for Ontario (1997-2004). He holds a degree in Economics from Roanoke College in Virginia, and a Masters of Divinity from Covenant Theological Seminary in St. Louis.

Since 2004 he has worked as a consultant and Executive Coach specializing in leadership issues. He also owns B&B's French Wine Club. In 2014 his book, "Building A Vision For Your Life" was published. In 2016 he started The Timothy Foundation to equip young leaders with a theological education.

He is married to his wonderful wife Debbie and has two sons, Bryan and Taylor.

End Notes

[i] The master of divinity (M.Div.) degree wasn't wasted on me. I know that God was holding on to me, and my life in Christ has nothing to do with my holding on to God. Yet there is still the human responsibility aspect; and while I would never negate the complete and sovereign will of God, I would also never negate the responsibility of man.

[ii] A "Say-So" is a time–usually at the end of a week of camp–when kids who have decided to believe in Christ are asked to stand up in front of their peers and proclaim their new found faith. I am not saying this is a bad thing in and of itself (although I believe there are some cautions with it) but I am making the point that this one time proclamation cannot be the "end in mind."

[iii] *The Story of Christianity*, Justo L. Gonzalez, vol. 1, p. 96.

[iv] It is interesting to note that the artists at the time of Michelangelo combined religion and biology in their art. The artist created works that reflected his beliefs and also reflected accurate biological research. They studied the human anatomy in order to paint or sculpt it.

[v] I believe we need to seriously reconsider our vocabulary when we talk about salvation. We do not "let Christ into our lives," or "give our lives to Christ," or even "open the door of our life to Christ," because these phrases indicate a work on our part. It is rather that Christ draws us to Himself in such a powerful way that all we can do is respond to His love for us. Perhaps a phrase more like "I responded to Christ" would be more accurate and helpful in our understanding of what actually happens in salvation.

[vi]*The 7 Habits of Highly Effective People*, Stephen R. Covy, 1989 Simon & Schuster, p. 71.

[vii] Recently I've written two devotional guides for Bible study. One is a daily study through the book of John and the other is a similar study through the book of Romans. These books contain questions for thought each day as well as a place to journal in prayer. What makes these study guides different from most others is that there is very little commentary. Most devotional guides tell you what to read, tell you what to think, and some even tell you what to pray. This creates passive Christians who do not learn the discipline of actively engaging the Biblical text for themselves and wrestling with the questions raised by the words of Scripture. We need to get kids reading and studying

the Scripture for themselves so that they are able to study it on their own long after they've left our ministry.

[viii] You may be thinking that you don't have the time to prepare a weekly alumni newsletter. Each week I was already preparing a Bible study for Campaigners and Leadership. I simply turned that study into a one-page summary for our Alumni Newsletter. We had a group of local college kids write the other side of the newsletter, assemble it, and mail it.

[ix] This is not to say that we do not play a role in proclaiming the Gospel. Jesus tells us in Matthew 28:19 to "Go therefore and make disciple of all the nations..." and Paul encourages the preaching of the Gospel in Romans 10: 14–15 saying, "How then shall they call on Him in whom they have not believed? And how shall they believe in Him of whom they have not heard? And how shall they hear without a preacher? And how shall they preach unless they are sent? As it is written: How beautiful are the feet of those who preach the Gospel of peace. Who bring glad tidings of good things!" My point is that although this principle—that Christians are called to proclaim the Word of God—is true, it is not the point being taught in this parable.

CPSIA information can be obtained
at www.ICGtesting.com
Printed in the USA
LVOW03s2233161017
552622LV00002B/213/P